BEGINNING WITH THE HANDICAPPED

DRESSING FOR THE HANDICAPPED

Second Printing

BEGINNING WITH THE HANDICAPPED

By

VERNA HART, Ed.D.

*Associate Professor
Coordinator, Program for
Early Childhood Education
for the Handicapped
University of Pittsburgh
Pittsburgh, Pennsylvania*

CHARLES C THOMAS · PUBLISHER
Springfield · Illinois · U.S.A.

Published and Distributed Throughout the World by

CHARLES C THOMAS ● PUBLISHER

Bannerstone House

301-327 East Lawrence Avenue, Springfield, Illinois, U.S.A.

© *1974, by* CHARLES C THOMAS ● PUBLISHER

ISBN 0-398-03179-7

Library of Congress Catalog Card Number: 74-5150

First Printing, 1974
Second Printing, 1978

With THOMAS BOOKS *careful attention is given to all details of
manufacturing and design. It is the Publisher's desire to present books that
are satisfactory as to their physical qualities and artistic possibilities and
appropriate for their particular use.* THOMAS BOOKS *will be true to those
laws of quality that assure a good name and good will.*

Printed in the United States of America
R-11

Library of Congress Cataloging in Publication Data

Hart, Verna.
    Beginning with the handicapped.
    1. Handicapped children--Care and treatment.
I. Title.
RJ135.H47   649'.15'1   74-5150
ISBN 0-398-03179-7

To parents who are the child's first teachers and
to teachers who are substitute parents.

FOREWORD

T HE FIRST MISTAKE made in working with a handicapped child is believing that a miracle will be wrought. The second mistake is believing that a miracle cannot be wrought. Neither expectation can be realized without an honest effort — and the effort never ceases.

Every child is entitled a chance to succeed to his maximum ability level. This level may vary from child to child, but every child, no matter how handicapped, can learn *something*. The task is to appropriately identify *what* to teach and then *how* to teach it. It is hoped that the suggestions that have been offered will be of help. Luck and best wishes to those who use them with patience, kindness, persistence and love.

INTRODUCTION

M OST OF THE SEVERELY handicapped children begin life behind their normal peers in many significant ways; there is no time to waste in teaching them the basic routines of life. Parents have the responsibility to toilet train, wean, and give their children other self-care skills. Teachers also share some of these responsibilities. But both the parents and the teachers are often unprepared because they do not know the sequential development of the low functioning, handicapped child.

Most parents are aware of an existing or forthcoming bowel movement in a young child; and, if he is a normal child, the parents know what to do. Whether the signal from the child is a grunt, a grimace, or a blush (a loved one once let us know in technicolor), the child is quickly on the potty chair. Soon, after a few successful experiences, the child thinks, "Boy! this sure beats a cold, icky diaper — and look how pleased mama is with me!" The severely handicapped child also has a comfort level and he too reacts favorably to a pleased parent or teacher. But how can we help him to quickly achieve success in this and other self-care areas?

This manual is one approach and is meant to be used in total as presented or adapted to a particular need. The philosophy has been developed through use with many children and is meant to help others save time by avoiding the many mistakes that were made through trial and error. It is built on the premise that all children can learn if the tasks are analyzed carefully enough and presented according to the child's level of development.

CONTENTS

BEGINNING WITH THE HANDICAPPED

WHERE TO BEGIN

THIS MANUAL GIVES specific ways to teach the child what he must learn. It is written with the purpose of changing the behavior of any specific child. In order to do this you first have to measure what the child is doing before you attempt to change him. *Find out what he can do right now.* When you know what he can do, you will know where to start teaching him what he can't do.

Another reason why it is important to know what the child is now doing is to compare and measure what he has learned. You can show his change in behavior to others who are interested in his progress, as well as to see what kind of a job you have done as his teacher.

What happens to a child *at the time* he does something is very important to him. If he likes what happens to him, he has been rewarded; if he doesn't like what happens to him, he has been punished or unrewarded. A child, like the rest of us, will repeat actions that give him rewards. Therefore, when a child does something that you want him to do, it is important to reward him for doing it — at the time he does it.

Each child responds to different kinds of rewards because every child, *as a person*, has his own likes and dislikes. When you are around a child long enough, you learn the things he likes best. These are usually praise or various kinds of physical contacts; things he can eat; things with which he can hold, wear, or play; privileges or physical activities; and, as he gets older, money. Rewards of praise and physical contacts are always available to us, and for that reason it is better to reward with a kiss and a hug or other signs of affection. Some children are not rewarded by this type of behavior. However, you can have this type of reward as a goal for the future. In the meantime, such things can be used as a bite of food that a child likes as a reward for taking a bite of food that he doesn't like. Often the best reward is one that the child chooses. The child somehow lets you know what he wants.

Remember that food may ruin the child's appetite, but sometimes food is the only reward that you can use at a particular time. If your child likes you to swing him around, you can use that as an initial reward. He must do what you want him to do first, and then you can reward him by swinging. Work? Time consuming? You bet it is! But think of your reward, the child's learning; so be a swinger for a while.

If the child receives a reward *at the time* he does what you want him to do, he knows for what he is being rewarded. This will make him want to repeat the action so he will get another reward. If you wait to reward a child, he may have done something in the meantime, and he'll think you are rewarding him for that behavior. It is important to reward immediately. Later, the child can learn to delay his reward, but at the beginning he needs to have you reward him as he carries out the activity.

Often it is surprising what acts as a reward to a child. You might be rewarding a behavior when you don't mean to. A child might bite because of the attention he gets. The attention he gets becomes his reward for biting. If this is the case, by ignoring this behavior, the child will no longer be rewarded, and the biting may stop. Spanking, yelling and slapping can all be rewards. They are not rewards to us, but they may be to others. A child may be willing to suffer a spanking because of the attention he gets.

You must make sure that you are not rewarding behavior that you want to extinguish. The best way to do this is to be positive and reward the child when he is doing something positive. Make sure you give him the attention that he wants *only when he is doing what you want him to*. Attention can be a very good reward, so you want to bestow it only when the child is performing the behavior you want. Be sure that you reward any good behavior that takes the place of any undesirable behavior.

In the beginning of an activity, reward the child each time

he does what you want. After a while you will not have to reward him each time. The correct behavior will last longer if he is only rewarded part of the time. Give the rewards only when the behavior gets better or gets closer to the behavior you want the child to have. If the child sat quietly for four minutes and had been rewarded, you would not reward him until he sits for four and one-half minutes the next time.

Your child will probably not begin by accepting a verbal reward as the one that works best with him. Children usually prefer a hug, piece of candy, or swing instead of your saying "good." Your goal is to condition him to accept the word *good* as a reward. The easiest way to teach this is to say the word each time you give him his preferred reward. The word *good* and your evident pleasure will eventually be reward enough. When we adults are told we have done a good job, we are very pleased; of course, that praise is our reward. This is what the goal should be for your child.

The first objective is usually that of obtaining behavior control of the child. If a child does not obey, it is difficult to teach him other behaviors. Therefore, get your child to respond to you and to what you ask of him. As the child follows your very first commands in this new adventure, reward him. *And reward him at the time he does it!* He will learn that doing what you ask is a rewarding experience, and he will try the other behaviors that you ask of him.

READINESS FOR AN ACTIVITY

In order for your child to be as independent as his capacity allows, you must push him to do as much for himself as possible. A preschool child can be very attractive and appealing in expressing his need to have things done for him. A teenager with the same need to have others care for his simplest desires is not attractive or appealing. Normal children learn to care for themselves in the preschool years, and you want to encourage your handicapped child to do as much as possible during this same period. Admission to the various programs for handicapped children often depends on such matters as toilet training, feeding, or dressing skills. If the child is already in a program that does accept those who are not able to care for themselves, the teaching time that could be spent on other activities is often spent on simple self-care. It is important to teach these skills as early and quickly as possible so the child can go on to other tasks.

When deciding whether a child is ready to learn a task, you must observe the child for clues to his readiness to begin training. A child who is dry all night and has two-hour periods of dryness during the day is ready for toilet training. The child who is never dry for any period of time is not ready. His bladder never gets full enough of urine to make him feel the need to empty it or the feeling of relief it gives him when he does empty it. Beginning toilet training too soon does nothing but frustrate the child and his parent or teacher.

If a child has not learned the simple movement of bringing his hand to his mouth, it is useless to try to teach independent spoon-feeding; he simply isn't ready. He may, however, be *ready to learn* to bring his hand to his mouth. If you dunk his fingertips into something sweet and then put his fingertips to his mouth, it may help him develop the hand-to-mouth movement he needs for the spoon-feeding that will come later.

You must really observe the child to see if he is ready to learn. Too often it appears as if a child can do nothing, when actually there are a number of things he can do. Parents and teachers may look at their child repeatedly, but not really see him. Perhaps you may think a child never sits still; yet he might be sitting still for long periods of time. You could prove it if you carried around a stopwatch and noted his quiet minutes.

You can reduce the period of time it takes for a child to learn something if you move him through each step of an activity. Rather than pulling up a child's pants for him, you can stand behind him, place your hands over his, and have him pull up his own pants with your hands doing the work but with his going through the actual movements. By doing this, he has fewer new movements to learn, and you can withdraw your hands during any phase of a movement pattern as he performs it himself.

If you have always fed a child by sitting across from him, he learns to feel the spoon coming in from that angle. He may then struggle or refuse food when you try to get him to feed himself because the spoon will be coming from a different angle and will feel strange to him. Therefore, you want to begin the actual self-feeding movement as soon as you see that he is ready. When his hand-to-mouth movements are such that he shows he can get things to his mouth with a steady movement and he can hang on to something with a good grasp, he is showing his readiness. It is at this time that you begin to put him through the feeding process of putting your hand over his and guiding the food to his mouth.

TEACHING A TASK

If a child has not yet learned to take care of any of his needs, the best place for you is to assume a position behind him with your body facing his back. With this method, you can put the child through various movements and he can learn them in a natural way. He will learn how his muscles should feel as he carries out the task. Think of Arnold Palmer standing close behind you, showing you how to swing a golf club.

Have you, as an adult, ever been fed by someone? Try it. Have someone feed you and know how uncomfortable it is. The spoon comes in from the wrong direction; you can't get the food off the spoon without dripping, and you move your head to try to get the spoon at the right angle. A similar sensation can be experienced by a child who is learning to feed himself after he has always been fed from the front. Not only does he have to learn to pick up a spoon and feed himself, but he also has to learn the new feelings that accompany the very act of eating.

Stand, kneel or sit directly behind the child. Depending on the type of activity, place yourself in a kneeling position behind him or sit in a chair behind him with one leg on each side of his body. If he is sitting on the floor, sit with him between your spread legs. The closeness of your body and body warmth can be reassuring to him as you carry out the task. The vibrations of your speech can be especially comforting to a deaf or blind child. Also, your close body contact can lead to socialization for the child. You want him to learn to like people and to regard them as sources of comfort. He will learn that it is people who can meet his needs.

Place your hands directly over the child's. What you are trying to do is to have the child learn the movements of eating, dressing, bathing, etc. By placing your hand over his and putting him through the movements, you establish his learning pattern. Your goal is to have him carry out all of the activities by himself. At first you will be doing all the work, but he will still be going through every movement.

Move your hand to his wrist as soon as he shows that he can perform certain steps in the task without your holding his hand. You more or less guide him and act as a reminder when you have your hand at his wrist. At the same time that you guide his wrist, give him the verbal command for the movement you are giving him. "Scoop your food." "Lift up your spoon." "Turn on the faucet." These are all verbal commands that you can give the child as you direct his hands. Do not move your hands to his wrist until you are sure he can do that particular step in the task.

Move your hand to his elbow as soon as he is able to do a step of the learning task independently or give him only verbal directions if he has enough language ability to understand what you are saying. When you put your hand on his elbow, place it under the elbow and use your hand as a guide or reminder. Give him the verbal command as you guide his arm. "Drink your milk." "Use some soap." "Wash the backs of your hands." This step assumes that the child is able to do the task but may be distracted or become pokey in carrying it out. You are merely acting as a verbal or tactual (touch) reminder for him to get busy.

Many times the child will not or is not able to do the things you have chosen for him to do. For this reason it is best to put the child through the various movements he needs to know in order to carry out the activity by himself.

CHARTING THE BEHAVIOR

It often becomes very discouraging if a child takes a long

time to learn something that you are trying to teach him. This may be your fault, not the child's. You may have tried to teach him too much at one time. When adults learn typing, for example, they don't learn all the letters, their positions, the movements, and the spacers at one sitting. They learn in a simple step-by-step sequence; this is the way you must teach the child. You must analyze the task you are trying to teach and learn how you can break it down into simple steps. This is called a *task analysis approach*, and it is used throughout the manual. By using this approach each goal becomes an individual part of the total task. You divide the task into small steps so the child can easily learn one thing.

You need some way to show that the child is learning what you are trying to teach him; you measure what he has learned on a chart. This gives a record of what he has learned and how fast he has learned it.

The first column in the charts of task analysis used throughout this manual shows that the child can do the activity if you put your hands over his and put him through each step. Every step that you can move him through should be shown by coloring that step on the chart. Color in the squares with a magic marker or crayon. If you use a different color for different days or weeks, you will be able to determine how long it takes him to learn an activity. It the color shows he is staying on one step too long, the step may not be simple enough. You will have to analyze the task again and perhaps put in an additional step.

The second column in the task achievement chart shows that the child can do the particular step if you only guide his hand at the wrist. He can grasp his spoon by himself, but you may need to guide his hand by the wrist to his plate to help him fill the spoon.

As soon as a child can do the step in column 1, move to column 2. Each time column 1 is filled in, column 2 becomes the teaching task. The child may have spotty charts; that is to be expected. Your task is to always fill the columns in order from left to right with the goal the last column on the right.

Column 3 is filled in when the child is able to carry out

the step by himself but needs an occasional reminder. This reminder can be verbal — you tell him what to do — or it can be tactual — you help him a little by guiding his elbow in the right direction.

Column 4 indicates that the child can do the step all by himself. He has learned one part of the whole and has become a little more independent. When all the steps of one activity have column 4 filled in, the child will be able to carry out that complete task by himself.

This is an example of how you can use the charts.

	Your hand over his	Your hand on his wrist	Verbal or tactual reminder	He does task by himself
Drinks liquid from a cup				

By filling in column 1, you indicate that you have to hold the cup for him while he drinks. Your goal is to fill in column 2. Try to get him to hold the cup in his own hands, but help him by holding his wrist and guiding his hands to get the cup to his mouth. Be patient, accept messy accidents, and be loving.

	Your hand over his	Your hand on his wrist	Verbal or tactual reminder	He does task by himself
Drinks liquid from a cup	////////			

Filling in column 2 indicates that the child is able to grasp the cup and get it to his mouth with your help on his wrists.

The next goal, column 3, is to see if he can get the cup to his mouth with perhaps just a little guidance of his arms or with a verbal reminder such as, "That's a boy. Get it up to your mouth." When he can do this step, you fill in column 3; column 4 then becomes your goal. This is when he solos and you both thrill to his achievement.

By filling each column with a different color and marking the corresponding days on a calendar, you will know how long it took to accomplish each step on the chart: column 1, blue for October 18 to October 25; column 2, red for October 25 to November 8; column 3, green for November 8 to November 28; and in column 4 you would write November 29. Therefore, it took six weeks to learn this step.

Make sure there are no blank columns in each step of the task.

	Your hand over his	Your hand on his wrist	Verbal or tactual reminder	He does task by himself
Drinks liquid from a cup	Blue	Red	Green	Nov. 29
Calendar key	10/18-10/25	10/25-11/8	11/8-11/28	

CHAPTER 2

SELF-CARE SKILLS

TOILET TRAINING

TOILETING A CHILD is too often viewed as a difficult task by both parents and teachers. Sometimes a child may be refused admission to an educational program because he is not toilet trained. The parent tries again and again to "housebreak" the child and adds even more to the emotional strain. The parent is determined that the child will become trained; the child, sensing the emotional undertones, refuses to cooperate.

Toilet training should be as unemotional to the child *and* the parent or teacher as eating, drinking and dressing. If this task is approached by taking the various steps of going to the toilet one at a time the goal will be reached more quickly.

A child needs to reach a certain level of maturity before he can be trained. *Children differ in their ages when they reach this stage.* The best way to determine this level of maturity is by noting the time period before he wets or soils himself. The dry period should be about two hours long: he will then have the feeling of a full bladder and will know the sensation of relief as he empties his bladder. The praise he receives when he urinates, plus the feeling of relief he has, will help him know why you are putting him on the toilet.

If the child is small, a potty chair should be used to allow him to sit comfortably with his feet on the floor. Many children do not like their feet dangling in space. A child may also feel afraid of falling through a large toilet seat (and he could). Small seats with a urine shield that fits over the regular toilet seat can be used with a step stool for the child's feet. This will aid independence.

Independence is important in toileting; the child must be able to take care of his needs by himself. At first, when he begins to be dry, he will not be able to hold his urine for long intervals. If he has to wait each time for someone to lift him up to place him on the toilet, accidents will happen. Some accidents will happen irregardless. It's important that you accept them and not lose your equanimity (cool). You should know, and so should the child, that a toilet accident is not bad, dirty, naughty, or a no-no. It is simply an accident without blame. The more the child is able to gauge his timing with his holding ability, the fewer the accidents.

It is better to have the toileting time set up by the child rather than a specific time when you hope to catch him. A chart should be kept for a few days to see when the child usually urinates and defecates. The time should be noted for each, because both functions should show some kind of pattern.

Charts, such as the one illustrated (p. 14) can be used and checked during the child's waking hours. It's a bother and it takes time to check the child each ten minutes during the day, but three or four days of effort will shorten the time and ease your task once the actual training is begun.

After you have kept a chart for three or four days, a pattern will appear *if* the child is ready for training. There should be clustered periods when the child is dry and when he is wet or soiled. A chart may look like the one on page 19.

The best time to begin your training is *after a pattern appears* and at a time when the behavior is most likely to occur. In the example illustrated, 10:10 was the earliest the child urinated in the five days checked. If you put the child on the potty at 10:10, chances of success are much greater. For the best progress, always place the child on the potty at the earliest time charted in each grouping. If one time is noted at an unusual period, ignore it because you are trying to find a time when you will have the most success. In the illustration, 11:20 was charted only once. The weather, excitement and temperature can all contribute to irregularities in the charts. Because these are usually temporary, they are not considered when making up your toilet schedule.

A two-hour period of dryness between charted clusters will

Urinating (U) and Bowel Movement (BM) Chart

a.m.	Sun.	Mon.	Tues.	Wed.	Thurs.	Fri.	Sat.
6:00							
6:10							
6:20							
6:30							
6:40							
6:50							
7:00							
7:10							
7:20							
7:30							
7:40							
7:50							
8:00							
8:10							
8:20							
8:30							
8:40							
8:50							
9:00							
9:10							
9:20							
9:30							
9:40							
9:50							

a.m.	Sun.	Mon.	Tues.	Wed.	Thurs.	Fri.	Sat.
10:00							
10:10							
10:20							
10:30							
10:40							
10:50							
11:00							
11:10							
11:20							
11:30							
11:40							
11:50							
NOON							
12:10							
12:20							
12:30							
12:40							
12:50							
1:00							
1:10							
1:20							
1:30							
1:40							
1:50							
2:00							
2:10							

p.m.	Sun.	Mon.	Tues.	Wed.	Thurs.	Fri.	Sat.
2:20							
2:30							
2:40							
2:50							
3:00							
3:10							
3:20							
3:30							
3:40							
3:50							
4:00							
4:10							
4:20							
4:30							
4:40							
4:50							
5:00							
5:10							
5:20							
5:30							
5:40							
5:50							
6:00							
6:10							

p.m.	Sun.	Mon.	Tues.	Wed.	Thurs.	Fri.	Sat.
6:20							
6:30							
6:40							
6:50							
7:00							
7:10							
7:20							
7:30							
7:40							
7:50							
8:00							
8:10							
8:20							
8:30							
8:40							
8:50							
9:00							
9:10							
9:20							
9:30							
9:40							
9:50							
10:00							
10:10							
10:20							

p.m.	Sun.	Mon.	Tues.	Wed.	Thurs.	Fri.	Sat.
10:30							
10:40							
10:50							
11:00							
11:10							
11:20							
11:30							
11:40							
11:50							
MIDNIGHT							

insure greater success in toilet training. This two-hour period insures a bladder full enough for the child to experience a great feeling of relief when he urinates. When he experiences this, he will get the meaning of what you are trying to get him to do.

When you have determined the most likely time for success, take your child to the bathroom. He must learn that this is a behavior that takes place in a certain setting. Placing the potty in the bathroom and keeping it there means that he will not have to unlearn something later on. If your child is large enough to use the regular toilet, use it. This, too, will prevent having to learn a new setting for the task.

When you decide to start toilet training, remove the diapers and put training pants or shorts on your child; it also helps to say a little prayer, take a deep breath, and cross your fingers.

Training pants are simple to get off in a hurry and easier for the child to push down himself. By not using rubber pants the child quickly knows when he has gone and is more uncomfortable when his pants are cold and wet. Using the toilet, then, becomes even more comforting and rewarding.

Take your child to the bathroom and stand or kneel behind him. Place your hands on his and help him push down his pants and undershorts. Then seat him on the toilet or potty. Five minutes is long enough the first time you seat him there. You will *gradually* make this time longer if he does not urinate or move his bowels. Remember, the time he sits there should not be longer than the cluster of times you have checked on your charts.

Toileting too often becomes a battlefield between parent or teacher and child. Any toileting attempt should be matter-of-fact, and the child should know that he is to sit there. Do not do anything to make him think he is being punished or that it is simply a game-time. He is there for one purpose, to empty his bladder or bowels. Be serious and be kind; he will get the message.

If the child tries to get up or cries when you put him on the potty, hold him firmly, but gently, until he stops struggling. Re-

Urinating and Bowel Movement Chart

a.m.	Sun.	Mon.	Tues.	Wed.	Thurs.	Fri.	Sat.
10:00							
10:10	U				U		
10:20			U				
10:30		U/BM					
10:40							
10:50							
11:00							
11:10							
11:20				U			
11:30							

lease your hold only after he has stopped struggling for a few seconds. Let him get up only when he is quiet. Otherwise, he will get the idea that crying or struggling will get him his reward; that is, being allowed off the toilet.

If the child does urinate or have a bowel movement, reward him by showing how pleased you are. Hug him, clap, laugh, or do anything that has reinforced him in the past.

Stay with the child all the while he is on the potty. Only by rewarding him at the time he urinates or has his bowel movement will he know *why* you're rewarding him. It will help to talk, read or interact with him while you are waiting for him. This will help him to relax, and your chances of success will be greater. The interaction should be kept low-key; excitement or the child's feeling that it is nothing but game-time will lower your chances of success.

If the child has had a bowel movement, the next step is to put your hand over his and locate the toilet paper. Help him roll off a piece, tear it, fold it and wipe himself. You will need to take care as your teach him to wipe himself, because he will not be able to see what he is doing and will have to learn by touch.

Girls present particular problems when they are being taught to wipe themselves. They must be very careful not to spread the germs from the stool or anus to their vagina. Bladder and kidney infections can be caused by improper wiping. When teaching wiping with your hand over the girl's hand, go from front to back (vagina to anus), *never* back to front. If the girl has only urinated, a blotting motion is sufficient. Next, with your hand still on the child's, discard the paper by dropping it into the toilet. When a boy urinates it is important not to restrict the force of the flow of urine by pressure against his penis with his fingers. The few drops or urine that can remain in his penis because of this pressure may drip on him or his clothing.

After the child is finished he should stand up and turn to flush the toilet. Sometimes the flushing motion and sound it makes will act as a reward for using the toilet.

With your hands over his, pull up the child's pants if he

has not yet learned this as part of his dressing skills. Then lead him to the sink and have him wash his hands. By teaching him to wipe himself, flush the toilet, and wash his hands, toileting becomes a complete act.

If the child does not urinate or have a bowel movement while he is on the toilet, do not punish him and do not reward him. Wait until the next cluster of times you have marked on your charts, then try again. In the meantime, remember all the things that can be rewarding to your child. If you play with him each time you change his dirty pants, it can be more rewarding for him not to be toilet trained.

A child may show many signs of being ready to be toilet trained. He may have already been "caught" by a parent or teacher who has placed him on the potty at regularly scheduled times. He may be "caught" because of the physical signs he shows — squirming, holding himself, becoming very quiet, blushing, etc. He may show discomfort after he has wet or soiled his pants. When you keep a chart on a child who shows such signs, you will usually observe the longer periods of time when he is dry. You can pinpoint the approximate time when he will be urinating or having a bowel movement and then watch the signs for the exact time he needs to be placed on the toilet. You will then have even greater success by taking advantage of both the charts and his signs.

HAND WASHING

Hand washing begins with your hand over the child's and by putting him through all of the steps. Move your hand to his wrist as quickly as the child shows he can do a step by himself. Go to the tactual reminder by gently guiding his elbow or verbally telling him what he should be doing.

A child seldom learns the whole hand washing task in sequence. He may be able to reach for a towel independently before he can do anything else. Remember, let him carry out each step by himself as soon as he shows he can do it. Do not help him with any step that he is able to do himself, but put him through the whole task in sequence every time.

The child:	Your hand over his	Your hand on his wrist	Verbal or tactual reminder	He does task by himself
1. Find bathroom				
2. Enters bathroom				
3. Locates door				
4. Shuts door				
5. Finds toilet				
6. Pulls down pants				
7. Sits on toilet				
8. Uses toilet				
9. Reaches for paper				
10. Rolls out paper				
11. Tears off paper				
12. Folds paper				
13. Cleans himself				
14. Drops paper in toilet				
15. Stands up				
16. Locates toilet handle				
17. Flushes toilet				
18. Pulls up pants				
19. Fastens waist of pants				
20. Pulls top over waist				
21. Finds sink				
22. Washes hands				
23. Opens door				
24. Leaves bathroom				

FACE WASHING

A procedure similar to hand washing is used to wash the

face. Temperature regulation of the water is necessary for washing the face, while cold water alone can be used for hand washing. A washcloth must also be used; squeezing the water out of the washcloth can be a complicated task for some children. Remember, let the child carry out the steps he can by himself and help only with those he cannot do.

The child:	Your hand over his	Your hand on his wrist	Verbal or tactual reminder	He does task by himself
1. Finds sink				
2. Finds faucets				
3. Turns on water				
4. Wets one hand				
5. Wets two hands				
6. Finds soap				
7. Picks up soap				
8. Soaps hands				
9. Replaces soap				
10. Rinses hands				
11. Finds faucets				
12. Turns off water				
13. Finds towel				
14. Dries hands				
15. Hangs up towel, or				
16. Finds wastebasket				
17. Throws away towel				

The child:	Your hand over his	Your hand on his wrist	Verbal or tactual reminder	He does task by himself
1. Locates sink				
2. Finds faucets				
3. Turns on cold water				
4. Turns on hot water				
5. Regulates water temperature				
6. Finds and takes washcloth				
7. Wets washcloth				
8. Squeezes water from cloth				
9. Finds soap				
10. Grabs soap				
11. Soaps wash cloth				
12. Replaces soap				
13. Washes face, eyes closed				
14. Rinses cloth under faucet				
15. Wrings out cloth				
16. Rinses face				
17. Rinses cloth				
18. Locates towel rod				
19. Hangs up washcloth				
20. Turns off water				
21. Locates towel				
22. Takes towel				
23. Rubs face dry				
24. Replaces towels				

BRUSHING TEETH

Your child will be able to do some of the toothbrushing

steps before he will be able to do others because various kinds of skills are needed — twisting to get the top off the toothpaste tube, spitting, brushing, etc. Make sure that you do not do anything for the child that he can do for himself.

Standing behind the child, put him through all of the movements involved in toothbrushing. Remove your help for the steps the child can carry out himself.

NOSE CARE

Wiping his nose is one of the tasks that makes your child acceptable to other people. You teach this task in the same way as the others; by putting him through the movements and gradually removing your help so that he learns the activity independently.

The child:	Your hand over his	Your hand on his wrist	Verbal or tactual reminder	He does task by himself
1. Places tissue over nose				
2. Wipes nose with tissue				
3. Blows nose				
4. Blows and wipes nose simultaneously				
5. Throws away used tissues				
6. Covers nose and mouth when sneezing				
7. Covers nose and mouth when coughing				

EATING

If the child needs a special spoon or an aid such as a cylinder-shaped block taped to the spoon handle to help him grasp it, make sure that he uses it *each time* he eats. This is a part of being consistent when you establish his eating habits.

Before you begin to teach feeding to the child, observe

The child:	Your hand over his	Your hand on his wrist	Verbal or tactual reminder	He does task by himself
1. Finds sink				
2. Locates and grasps toothpaste				
3. Turns cap off paste				
4. Puts cap down				
5. Locates and grasps brush				
6. Squeezes paste on brush				
7. Puts toothpaste tube down				
8. Places brush in mouth				
9. Brushes front teeth and left back teeth up and down and back and forth				
10. Turns wrist and brushes right back teeth up and down and back and forth				
11. Spits out toothpaste				
12. Locates cold water faucet				
13. Turns on water				
14. Rinses brush				
15. Brushes teeth to rinse				
16. Rinses brush				
17. Brushes teeth to rinse				
18. Spits				
19. Rinses brush				
20. Returns brush to holder				
21. Wipes mouth with water				

him to see exactly what he is able to do. You will then know where to begin.

1. Can he hold up his head to eat?

	Your hand over his	Your hand on his wrist	Verbal or tactual reminder	He does task by himself
22. Locates faucet				
23. Turns off water				
24. Grasps toothpaste and cap				
25. Replaces cap				
26. Puts toothpaste away				
27. Locates towel				
28. Wipes mouth with towel				
29. Wipes hands on towel				
30. Replaces towel				

2. Can he hold food in his mouth until he swallows it?

3. Can he chew solid food?

Propping his head may be necessary before feeding. If the child is spending all his energy holding up his head, he has no strength left to eat.

Swallowing

Be sure the child is able to swallow before you try to teach him to feed himself. If the child is not able to swallow voluntarily, begin to teach this by using liquids the child enjoys. Fill the cup full enough so the child does not have to tip his head backwards to get the liquid. Help him hold his head slightly downward so he has to use his muscles for swallowing and is not just letting the liquid run down his throat. Put the edge of the cup just back of the teeth, but on top of the tongue. This is to keep the child from pushing the cup away with his tongue and from closing his teeth together to keep the liquid from going into his mouth. Keep the child from biting the cup.

After the liquid enters his mouth, make sure his lips are closed so it will not come back out again. Swallowing is also easier with the lips closed. If the child is not able to keep his mouth closed, sit directly behind him and cup his chin in your hand. Your little finger can hold the jaw shut, and your first two fingers can hold the lips shut. This leaves your other hand free to use the cup and to gently stroke his throat to encourage swallowing.

Give the child just a sip at a time and make sure that he swallows before you give him another. Otherwise he may choke.

If the child resists the cup by stiffening and turning his head, wait until he relaxes and then try again. This is the way he will learn that he gets food *only* when he relaxes. Remember, you are smarter, bigger and stronger than he is. It is also assumed that you have more patience.

Holding Food in the Mouth

A child who has not learned to use his tongue and lips may have trouble keeping food in his mouth long enough to swallow it. Good tongue and lip movements are necessary for good eating habits; they must also be developed before the child can produce good speech sounds. It is vital, then, that parents and teachers help the child establish these movements.

Holding the child's lips together as described for liquids can also help him keep food in his mouth. He needs to learn how to move food from the front of his mouth to his throat so he can swallow it. Up and down tongue movement must be developed instead of the in and out pushing movement that many children have.

At first it may be necessary to place the food midway back on the tongue. As the child develops the movement to make his food go back, food can be placed closer to the front of the mouth.

When teaching the child to move food within his mouth, soft foods should be used in the beginning. Applesauce, scrambled eggs, mashed potatoes, etc., are foods that can be swallowed without chewing, but they are foods that have enough consistency to aid the child in developing the kind of movement he needs.

Chewing

Up and down tongue movement is also needed for good chewing. Each time the teeth come together, the tongue should lift the food and put it up on the teeth's surface to be chewed again. With most children this is an automatic action. With the low-functioning child however, this ability may come only after a time of practicing. Begin to teach chewing by working the child's jaws in an up and down direction to give the child the idea of chewing. Place his hand on your face to give him the movement you want.

It is best to teach chewing by using semisolid foods. Small curd cottage cheese, fork-mashed vegetables, scrambled eggs with crumbled bacon, and chunky applesauce can all be used.

Place the food inside the child's mouth. Do not let him spit it out. Placing your hand in a cupping position under his chin with your fingers holding his lips together may be necessary. If he spits the food out, be calm and put another spoonful in. Gently massage his jaw to give him the chewing motion. Do not put more food in his mouth until the first spoonful is swallowed. It may be necessary for you to place your finger inside the child's lips and along his jaw to push food onto the chewing surfaces of the teeth. Be careful as you attempt this, however. Some children who refuse to bite food do very well when fingers are presented.

A swallow of milk or bite of some favorite food such as applesauce can be used as a reward for the child's chewing his food. A chewed bite of food can be followed by a bite of reward food.

Beginning to teach a child to chew can be very time-consuming, especially if the child has been on a bottle for a prolonged period. It is much easier to begin with a young child so he will learn to accept the feel of the different textures of food. Adequate amounts of protein foods are particularly needed for the development of both mind and body. Good chewing leads to the child's developing good speech as well as to the adequate intake of food for his intellectual development.

When beginning your feeding program, *no food should be given between meals! Bottles should be discontinued!* If the child is hungry, he will be more willing to eat. If the only food offered has to be chewed, the child will learn to chew. Again, consistency is important. If you decide it is time for the child to learn to chew solid foods, it is important that you keep to your decision. The first few days will be hard for you and for the child. Stick with it, and don't give up. Experience has shown that the method does work, and the results are worth the effort.

Self-feeding

Before the child can feed himself, he should be able to hold his head up, hold food in his mouth, swallow, and chew. He also must be able to bring his hand to his mouth. If he is not able to do this, he should be taught the movement. He already has this movement if he sucks his thumb, puts things in his mouth to explore, or if he bites his nails. If he does not have the movement, put his fingers in honey, jelly, pudding, etc., and guide his fingers to his mouth. Gradually withdraw your guidance and let the child direct his own hand-to-mouth movement. Finger foods such as cookies, crackers and toast can be used if he likes these foods and if he is able and willing to hold them.

FINGER-FEEDING. Finger foods should be used before teaching spoon behavior. This is the way to be sure that the hand to mouth movement is firmly established. The child also learns that he can bring food to his mouth himself. An exception to teaching finger-feeding first is when a child refuses to touch food with his hands. In this instance, spoon behavior would begin before finger-feeding; that is, if the hand-to-mouth movement has been established.

Begin finger-feeding by breaking food into small pieces and offering a piece to the child. If he does not direct the food to his mouth, sit behind him, put your hand over his, and direct the food to his mouth.

Drinking from a Glass

A firm plastic glass is best to teach drinking behavior be-

The child:	Your hand over his	Your hand on his wrist	Verbal or tactual reminder	He does task by himself
1. Directs food to his mouth to eat				
2. Holds food and then directs to mouth				
3. Picks up pieces of food and directs to mouth				
4. Bites off pieces of finger foods				

cause there is no risk of breakage. Follow the directions for holding liquids in the mouth and swallowing. Once the child can do this, put him through the movements of holding and drinking from a glass.

The child:	Your hand over his	Your hand on his wrist	Verbal or tactual reminder	He does task by himself
1. Drinks from a glass while you hold it				
2. Lifts the glass off table, two hands				
3. Lifts glass, drinks, returns to table				
4. Lifts glass with one hand				
5. Lifts glass with one hand, tilts to drink				
6. Lifts glass, drinks and returns to table — all with one hand				

Eating with a Spoon

Spoon usage is a continuation of the hand-to-mouth movement and of finger-feeding. When the spoon is introduced, wrap the child's hand around the handle and put your hands over his. Work from in back of him and guide his hand to his mouth. Begin spoon-feeding with foods that stick to the spoon so the child will get food each time he directs the spoon to his mouth. Foods like mashed potatoes, puddings, and peanut butter can be used.

For a blind child or for a child who has difficulty filling his spoon, direct his other hand for use as a pusher. One hand should grasp and direct the spoon while the other pushes food onto it. This will help him to know the amount of food on the spoon and will ensure that a loaded spoon is carried to his mouth to act as a reward for his action. As the child matures, a spoon, knife, or piece of bread can be used as pushers.

The child:	Your hand over his	Your hand on his wrist	Verbal or tactual reminder	He does task by himself
1. Holds spoon handle across palm				
2. Eats from a spoon				
3. Fills the spoon				
4. Eats without spilling				
5. Bites, puts spoon down, chews				
6. Holds spoon handle with thumb and fingers				
7. Distinguishes spoon from finger food				

Eating with a Fork

Learning to use a fork is similar to eating with a spoon. After the child has learned to fill a spoon and eat with it without spilling, he can learn to use a fork. At first he will use the fork as he uses the spoon. In time he will learn to use the fork for piercing food. He will also learn that certain foods such as puddings are easier to eat with a spoon than with a fork. Brief suggestions from you, such as "Try using your fork. It may be easier." Or, "Ice cream is easier to eat with a spoon," can help your child to learn which utensil to use with different foods.

Don't rush your child into using a fork. Make sure that he has good use of the spoon or you may confuse him by offering another tool for feeding himself.

The child:	Your hand over his	Your hand on his wrist	Verbal or tactual reminder	He does task by himself
1. Holds fork, handle across palm				
2. Eats from a fork				
3. Fills the fork				
4. Spears food with fork				
5. Eats without spilling				
6. Bites, puts fork down, chews				
7. Holds fork between thumb and fingers				
8. Distinguishes fork from spoon foods				

Eating with a Knife

Knife usage comes much later than the spoon, and spreading with a knife comes before cutting with one. Begin to teach spreading behavior by putting a glob of soft food such as jelly, butter or mayonnaise in the center of a piece of bread. Have the child grasp the knife handle. Place your hand over the child's and move the knife in a spreading motion. After he has learned to spread independently, teach him to cut meat "Continental Style." In this way the child holds the meat with his fork, tines down, in his left hand. He cuts with the knife held in his right hand by a gentle back and forth sawing motion. He then picks up the meat with the fork still in the left hand and still with the tines down. He thus brings the fork to the mouth. It is best to start with food that can be cut easily, as well as food the child likes so he is eager to use the cutting technique.

By teaching this method, it is not necessary to switch silverware from hand to hand and confuse the child. The fewer movements needed to teach an activity, the easier it is to teach.

The child:	Your hand over his	Your hand on his wrist	Verbal or tactual reminder	He does task by himself
1. Holds the knife for spreading				
2. Spreads bread				
3. Scoops spread and places on bread				
4. Holds knife for cutting				
5. Has sawing motion				
6. Holds meat with fork				
7. Holds with fork, cuts with knife				
8. Picks up food with fork and eats				

Using a Napkin

Each child should be taught the use of a napkin from the beginning of his self-feeding experience. Because he will use his hand as a food pusher, he needs to know that his hands should be wiped on a napkin and not on his clothes, the tablecloth, or you. It may be necessary to have several napkins available when the child is starting. His first efforts will be messy indeed. Dry washcloths can be used at first; the rough surfaces can rub off food, absorb liquids, and not stick to his hands as some paper napkins are apt to do. Washcloths can also easily be rinsed and used again.

The child:	Your hand over his	Your hand on his wrist	Verbal or tactual reminder	He does task by himself
1. Unfolds napkin				
2. Places napkin on lap or tucks in at neck or belt				
3. Wipes hands on napkin when needed				
4. Wipes mouth				
5. Places napkin on table when finished				

Pouring

Complete independence is the goal for each child. He needs to learn those skills that will help him to function in whatever setting he is in. A child at home needs to pour milk from a bottle or pitcher. A child at school must learn to open a milk carton and pour from it. Institutional settings often demand use of trays and cafeteria lines.

Working from behind the child with your hands over his, he can learn to open a milk carton. If he has poor vision or visual perception, it may help to place his fingers over the edge of the glass on the inside. He can pour the milk over his fingers to know if he is getting the milk on the inside of the glass. He will also learn when he has a full glass, because the milk rising to the tips of his fingers will signal him to stop pouring.

Using a Straw

The use of a straw gives a child good practice in using the muscles that help produce good speech. A hard plastic straw is preferable because the sides will not flatten together. After the child has learned to use the hard plastic straw, a soft plastic can

The child:	Your hand over his	Your hand on his wrist	Verbal or tactual reminder	He does task by himself
1. Pours drink from pitcher or bottle				
2. Pours drink from carton				
3. Opens carton				
4. Opens carton, pours drink				
5. Pours without spilling				
6. Stops pouring without overflowing				

The child:

	Yes	No
1. Sucks through a hard, plastic straw		
2. Brings liquid part way up		
3. Sucks liquid into mouth		
4. Continues steady sucking		
5. Sucks through a soft plastic straw		
6. Sucks through a paper straw		

be used. After the child is sucking well, regular paper straws can be used.

Cafeteria Lines

If the child has to go through a cafeteria line, stand behind him with your hands over his. Guide him through the line and, still with your hands over his, help him carry the tray to his table. Repeat the process each time he goes through the line, withdrawing your help to the wrist or elbow as he becomes able to do steps of the activity.

If the child is blind, the position of food on the plate should

The child:	Your hand over his	Your hand on his wrist	Verbal or tactual reminder	He does task by himself
1. Picks up tray				
2. Slides tray along ledge				
3. Picks up silverware				
4. Picks up napkin				
5. Picks up filled plate				
6. Places plate on tray				
7. Places plate without spilling				
8. Picks up other items				
9. Feels for end of serving ledge				
10. Grasps edges of tray				
11. Lifts tray from serving ledge				
12. Holds tray parallel to floor				
13. Walks, carrying tray				
14. Feels for edge of table				
15. Slides tray onto table from the edge				
16. Locates seat				
17. Seats himself				

be given. Take the child's hand, hold it lightly over the food and tell him, "Here is the meat loaf, here are the potatoes, here are the carrots." When he learns to tell time, the position of hands on a clock can be used. "The meat loaf is at twelve o'clock, the carrots at four," etc.

DRESSING

Children learn to take off clothing before they learn to put it on because it is easier. You want to encourage the child to remove his clothes as well as to help you when you dress him.

By working from behind the child with your hands over his, he will learn the basic movements needed for dressing and undressing. It helps to put the child through each step of the dressing sequence as you dress him. He may learn to do one step independently before he does others and they may be out of the sequence listed. This is fine. Just remember to teach the next step in order.

Pants

When putting on pants, it is best to put the pants flat on the floor, front up, in front of the child. Sit with the child between your spread legs so that you can reach around him to help him. Have the waist of the trousers nearest the child. Having the pants flat on the floor helps him put his legs into them without the pant legs flopping and resisting his attempts.

With your hands over the child's, grasp the edge of the waistband and create an opening for the child to slip his leg into. Have his hands pull up the pant leg until his foot comes through the bottom. Then lift the other leg and slide it into the second pant leg, and pull up the second leg until the foot comes through. Help the child stand up. With your hands on his, pull up his pants, fasten the hook or button at the waist, and pull up the zipper. Help him only in those steps where it is needed.

Pullover Shirt

Again, work from behind the child as you teach this activity. Place your hand over his whenever possible so that you are getting the child to go through the exact movements needed to dress himself.

Place the shirt, front down, on the floor or bed. Help the child gather up the sides of the shirt. Put the shirt over the head and pull it down. Push one hand and arm through a sleeve. Push the second hand and arm through the remaining sleeve. Pull the shirt down over the chest.

When undressing, reverse the process.

The child:	Your hand over his	Your hand on his wrist	Verbal or tactual reminder	He does task by himself
1. Unhooks hook				
2. Unzips zipper				
3. Pushes pants down				
4. Pulls one leg out of pant leg				
5. Pulls other leg out of pant leg				
6. Grasps waist of trousers				
7. Puts one leg in pant leg				
8. Pulls pant leg over foot				
9. Puts second leg in pant leg				
10. Pulls pant leg over second foot				
11. Stands up				
12. Pulls up trousers				
13. Hooks hook or fastens button				
14. Zips zipper				

Coat

Children often will put a coat on backwards or upside down. Various techniques can be used to teach the child to overcome this, but the following is used as a method that is socially acceptable and can be used as the child gets older.

Stand behind the child. Place the coat, front up with the bottom facing you, on the floor, table or bed. Take the child's left hand in your left hand as he faces the coat. Grasp the right side of the coat at shoulder level with his left hand. Put his right hand and arm into the right sleeve. Take his right hand and grasp the left hand side of the coat. Put the left hand and

The child:	Your hand over his	Your hand on his wrist	Verbal or tactual reminder	He does task by himself
1. Pulls shirt up to shoulders				
2. Pulls one arm from sleeve				
3. Pulls second arm from sleeve				
4. Pulls shirt off over head				
5. Gathers up shirt				
6. Slips shirt over head				
7. Puts shirt into position for arms				
8. Puts one arm through sleeve				
9. Puts both arms through sleeve				
10. Pulls shirt down over chest				

arm in the left sleeve of the coat. Then, putting your hands on his as needed, pull the coat up on his shoulders.

Socks

This task can be difficult for a child because he must learn to pull the sock on with the heel down. To teach the task, place your hands over the child's and work from behind as he sits on the floor between your legs.

Gather up the sock with the child's thumbs inside the sock, keeping the heel side down. Place the sock completely over the toes, then pull it up over the heel and ankle in one smooth motion. As you have your hands over the child's, make sure you pull the sock up without twisting so that the heel is in the proper

The child:	Your hand over his	Your hand on his wrist	Verbal or tactual reminder	He does task by himself
1. Knows back of coat from front				
2. Grasps right side of coat with left hand				
3. Puts right hand in sleeve				
4. Holds coat with right hand				
5. Moves coat into position				
6. Puts left hand in sleeve				
7. Pulls coat up on shoulders				

position. We know that it is frustrating to adjust a twisted sock. Don't try it or let the child try. Take the sock off and start over if the sock is twisted.

When taking off the socks, slip the fingers inside the sock and slide it over the heel. Then pull the sock off from the toe.

Shoes

Shoes hold a fascination for young children and many like to put their feet into their parents' shoes. They also like to remove their own shoes. Let them practice in this way; it is a good learning experience and should be encouraged.

It may help to mark one of the shoes as an aid for the child to match the right foot. Red fingernail polish inside the right shoe and on his right thumb can be an aid that's fun.

Lacing

Lacing is another activity that children enjoy but must learn to do correctly. Tying two laces of different colors together to form a long lace can aid the child in seeing the alternating use of the laces.

Seat the child between your legs. Take the child's hands in

The child:	Your hand over his	Your hand on his wrist	Verbal or tactual reminder	He does task by himself
1. Pulls sock off toes				
2. Slips sock down over heel				
3. Slips sock down over ankle and heel				
4. Gathers up the sock, thumbs inside				
5. Keeps heel side down				
6. Puts toes into sock				
7. Pulls sock up over heel				
8. Pulls sock up over ankle				
9. Puts sock on without twisting				

yours and put the ends of the laces through the bottom holes from the outside in. Pull the laces completely through the bottom holes so that the two lengths are even. Cross the laces and put the ends through the next holes from the inside out. Cross the laces again and put the ends through the next holes. Continue until all the holes have been filled. Use the alternating colors to show the child how he must cross the laces and how each hole must be filled.

Tying

A child must have good hand and finger control before he will be able to tie his shoes. It is wise to not begin trying to teach this activity until you are sure the child is able to use his fingers well enough to learn the task. It is one of the last dressing tasks learned.

Place your hands over the child's and show him how to pull the laces to tighten them. Next show him how to make the first half-knot. Place one lace around the other and pull the ends of each to make an "X." Pull the ends of the laces until tight.

The child:	Your hand over his	Your hand on his wrist	Verbal or tactual reminder	He does task by himself
1. Takes off untied shoes when loosened				
2. Loosens and removes untied shoes				
3. Unties, loosens and takes off shoes				
4. Loosens laces to put shoes on				
5. Pulls on shoe				
6. Pulls laces to tighten				
7. Puts the right shoe on the right foot				

The child:	Your hand over his	Your hand on his wrist	Verbal or tactual reminder	He does task by himself
1. Puts laces through bottom holes from the outside in				
2. Pulls laces through evenly				
3. Crosses the laces				
4. Puts laces through holes from the inside out				
5. Laces correctly, crossing and lacing each hole in order				

Next, make a loop with the right hand lace. Loop the left hand lace over the thumb and push it through the loop to form the other half of the bow. Pull the bow tight. Forming the bow is the hardest part, and a child who lacks coordination may not be able to learn it. It may be necessary to teach him to make a loop with each hand, treat the loop as single laces, cross them into an "X," and pull one loop through.

The child:	Your hand over his	Your hand on his wrist	Verbal or tactual reminder	He does task by himself
1. Pulls laces tight				
2. Crosses the laces to form an "X"				
3. Puts the lower lace down through the "X"				
4. Pulls ends of lace to form a half knot				
5. Forms a loop with one of the laces				
6. Makes a loop around his thumb				
7. Pushes lace through loop				
8. Forms second half of bow				
9. Pulls bow tight				

Buttoning

Buttoning also requires good coordination. The smaller the buttons, the greater the coordination needed. Therefore, it is best to begin teaching buttoning with large buttons and loose buttonholes.

Working from behind the child, take his hands in yours. Spread the buttonhole with the thumb of one hand. Take the button between the thumb and forefinger of the other hand. Insert one edge of the button into the buttonhole. Push the button through the hole with the thumb and forefinger while pulling from the other side with the opposite thumb and forefinger.

When unbuttoning, reverse the steps.

Mittens and Gloves

Mittens are easier for a child to put on than gloves. It is better, therefore, to dress a child in mittens until he can learn to put on gloves.

Placing your hand over the child's hold the mitten in the child's hand. Slip the other hand part-way into the mitten. Separate the thumb and push it into the thumb of the mitten. Take the unmittened hand and pull the mitten on the rest of the way. Grasp the remaining mitten in the mittened hand and hold it while the unmittened hand is pushed part-way into the mitten. Guide the thumb in. Pull the mitten on the rest of the way.

When putting on gloves, the procedure is similar. Pull the gloves on part-way and put the fingers into the right locations. After the fingers are in place, slip the thumb into place and pull the glove on the rest of the way. Repeat with the other glove.

The child:	Your hand over his	Your hand on his wrist	Verbal or tactual reminder	He does task by himself
1. Holds mitten, thumb side down				
2. Slips hand part way into mitten				
3. Puts thumb into thumb hole				
4. Pulls mitten on rest of way				
5. Grasps second mitten				
6. Slips second hand part way into mitten				
7. Puts second thumb into thumb hole				
8. Pulls second mitten on rest of way				

MOTOR DEVELOPMENT

THE CHILD LEARNS A GREAT DEAL by being able to move about. Some experts say that a child first must have many gross and fine motor skills before academic learning can take place. That is, he must be able to do things like walk (a gross motor skill) and other things like grasp (a fine motor skill).

To help the child develop both gross and fine motor skills, the following ideas are offered. They cover a wide range of ability. First, you must decide where the child is functioning and then take him sequentially through the steps of each task. Determine where he is now by going through the various tasks to see what he can do and where he has trouble. These troubled areas become your teaching tasks.

Do not expect your child to master tasks that are not at his level of development. A child will usually develop gross movements before he develops fine movements; he learns to sit before he learns to grasp a small bead. He also develops main body movements before he learns to use his extremities; he learns to roll before he can use his fingers to pick up objects. These facts need to be kept in mind when developing a motor program for your child. The movements should progress from gross to fine and from the main body to extremities.

The child should be developing all of his senses along with motor development: auditory (hearing), visual (seeing), kinesthetic (muscle movement), tactual (touch) and olfactory (smell). Gustatory (taste) can be better developed when feeding skills are taught. Chewing is a motor skill that can be mastered at that time also.

Some of the same techniques can be used to teach motor development that were used in teaching eating skills. Working behind the child and putting him through the activities will give

46

him the kinesthetic feel that he will experience when he does a movement on his own. This technique can also eliminate some of the fears that children may have of new movements and experiences.

Talking with a child slowly, quietly, and in short, simple sentences tends to remove some of his fear and will help him understand what you are attempting to do. By describing each activity you also help him to develop language concepts. "Put your arm up," is a verbal direction that helps the child learn the name for his arm as well as the direction "up." Simple language should always be used to make sure the child understands the direction you are giving him. Many times children are not able to carry out an activity because they are not sure of the instructions.

Mirrors are a big help in teaching motor movements. Full-length mirrors are the best, and unbreakable mirrors should be used because of the possibility of breakage and injury to the child. Mirrors show the sighted child what he is doing. Your demonstrations will give him the idea of what he is to imitate, and the mirror will help him know whether he is doing it correctly.

Touch also aids the child in motor development. By touching the part of the body to be used, the child is able to identify the verbal label that goes with the body part. For some children, sight and sound signals are useless, and touching signals are the clues they must use to carry out directions.

Smelling the objects to be used in an exercise may also help the child to identify them and their use. All of the senses do not work at their best for severely handicapped children, so use as many of the senses as you can to help him to get the idea of what he is to do and the way he is to do it.

Again, when selecting an activity, make sure that you consider the child's sequential level of development. Do not decide he should learn to skip simply because a normal child his age is skipping. He will not be ready to learn to skip until he can hop on one foot, and he will not hop on one foot until he can stand on one foot. It is important to make sure the child has all the skills needed to complete an activity. If he does not have all the skills needed to achieve an activity, it should not be taught.

Children perform best when we are consistent in what we expect of them and also in the way we treat them. Just as we would be upset if our boss told us to set our own hours for work and gave us no guidelines for what he expected, a child also needs to know what we expect of him. A child who has spent a lot of time trying to reach a goal we have set for him will be frustrated if we drop that goal, just as we become disturbed if we have spent considerable effort on a report, and then our boss decides the report wasn't really necessary. Children do not have our experience in dealing with such contradictions; an effort to be consistent, not letting a child spend a lot of time on a task that is not in keeping with your goals, is of the utmost importance.

You *must* make your expectations clear to the child. All too often a child fails to achieve because no one has asked him to try an activity. Positive expectancy should be the rule rather than the idea of "He can't do that," or "That's too difficult for him." By sequentially guiding your child through tasks, he may surprise you and delight himself with his abilities.

Be aware of fatigue as you put your child through the movements. Exercises where you move the child physically through the action do not take as much energy as ones where he does the moving. A child who has had no physical activities will tire with even passive exercises. His fatigue point will become much higher, and his strength will grow with regularly scheduled exercises. Foster as much endurance as you can in your child, because active play is a part of normal childhood.

Many severely handicapped children have orthopedic problems. If this is the case with your child, check with your orthopedic doctor or physical therapist before beginning the exercises. He can give you exercises or check those given here to determine which are suitable for your child.

GROSS MOTOR MOVEMENTS
Beginning the Motor Program
Time should be set aside each day to carry out a motor

program with your child. Several short periods would be better than a long one. Four ten-minute periods are better than one forty-minute session. The child will be able to withstand longer periods after he has developed stamina and certain skills.

Schedule the time for your motor program around established activities so you and your child won't forget. One period might be held just before bath time.

A special place is not necessary for the exercises. The plain floor, carpet, rug, or a firm mat can all be used. Dress the child so he will be comfortable and able to move freely. If the child wears long pants, make sure the crotch is pulled up to allow him free leg movement. Shoes should be removed.

Begin with a few movements and gradually add to them as he shows more ability and endurance. Talk to your child as you put him through the movements and make the whole procedure fun. The child should view the process as play. It is play with a purpose, however; demand a little more effort from him each time.

Exercise-type routines are established to develop muscle control and freedom of movement. These may not emerge immediately, but they will over a period of time. Some children possess very few voluntary movements, and you may have to put your child through each of the activities. With some, you may be able to stand behind him as you did with the self-care skills. Other children, with needs that demand lying on the floor, will require you to assume that or other positions.

The same developmental order that a normal child follows in movement will be outlined. In this way the child can develop his motor movements in sequence.

Passive Movements

HEAD ROLL. Place the child on his back with his legs out straight and his hands at his side. Kneel above the child's head and place your hands on the sides of his head. Gently turn his head from side to side, touching each ear to the mat. Do not move the shoulders or the rest of his body. Talk to the child to let him know what you are going to do. (For example, "Turn right, turn left," or a rhythmic, "This way, and that way, and this way . . ." Always punctuate your directions with a pleased, "Good boy! That's the way!") As he aids you in turning his head, fade out the amount of help you give him until he is able to make the roll independently.

HEAD LIFT. Begin by having the child lie facedown with his legs out straight. Place one of your hands on the back of his head and one hand under his chin. Gently lift his head off the mat. His shoulders and chest should remain on the mat with only his head lifting. Gradually fade your support as the child becomes able to aid the movement. Complete independence is your goal.

Turn the child over on his back with his legs straight out. Kneeling above his head, place one hand behind the child's head and the other on his forehead. Gently lift the child's head so that his chin touches his chest. Gradually fade your help as he learns to move independently.

HEAD LIFT AND FRONT ROLL. Combine the first two exercises. Place your hands on the sides of his head. Touch the chin to the chest as you repeat the head roll exercise. Fade your efforts as soon as possible.

ARM AND LEG MOVEMENTS. A young child moves both arms and legs together before he learns to move them independently of each other. Therefore, the child should be put through bilateral movements that use both his legs or arms at the same time before he is put through alternating or unilateral movements.

BILATERAL MOVEMENTS. Place the child on his back. The legs should be straight out with the legs relaxed and knees straight but not stiff. Kneel above or at the foot of the child and move him through the following positions:

Raise the child's arms with his elbows straight from his sides to touch his ears. Then move them back to his sides. Grasp the child's feet. Move his legs apart as far as they will go; then move his legs together again.

Grasp his ankle and wrist on one side of his body. Move his leg as far out as it will go and at the same time move the child's arm up so that it touches his ear. Coordinate the movements smoothly.

Fade your efforts as soon as possible.

Before a child learns to creep or walk, he must learn to move his arms and legs alternately to maintain his balance. Kneeling beside the child, put him through the following alternating movements:

The child should be lying on his back. With his elbows straight, move his arm until it touches his ear. Return it to his side. Do the same with his other arm. Continue the exercise, alternating the arms.

With the legs straight, spread one as far as it will go. Return it to position. Do the same with the other leg. Alternate the legs.

After the child is able to alternate arm and leg movements independently, he can perform simple body exercises using his arms and legs. Remember to use simple speech while the child does his exercises so he can attach the concept to the movement.

Have the child lie on his back.

1. From his side, put his arms together over his head.
   Speech: "Up, down"

2. Alternate his arms overhead.
   Speech: "Right arm up, down"
   "Left arm up, down"

3. Cross his arms over his body.
   Speech: "Right arm over, back"
   "Left arm over, back"

4. Arms in front straight up in the air.
   Speech: "Right arm up, down"
   "Left arm up, down"

5. Arms together in front.
   Speech: "Both arms up, down"

6. Leg lifts — one leg at a time, knee straight.
   Speech: "Right leg up, down"
   "Left leg up, down"

7. Leg lifts — both legs.
   Speech: "Both legs up, down"

8. Leg crossover — the left leg is straight and the right leg
   over and touches the floor.
   Speech: "Right leg up, over, touch, back down"
   "Left leg up, over, touch, back down"

9. Arm and leg lifts — bilateral.
   Speech: "Right arm and right leg up, down"
   "Left arm and left leg up, down"

10. Arm and leg lifts — alternating.
    Speech: "Right arm and left leg up, down"
    "Left arm and right leg up, down"

11. Arms and legs together.
    Speech: "Both arms, both legs up, down"

It is important to use the words "right" and "left" as you
give your instructions. Touch the child's correct arm or leg so he
will gradually associate the words with the appropriate limbs.
Actual knowledge of right and left will come much later, but this
is a good introduction to the terms.

Body Rolls

A child learns to roll from his stomach to his back before he
rolls from his back to his stomach because it is easier. Begin,
then, to teach the child to turn from his stomach to his back.

The roll is made possible because of the relation between
the shoulder and the hips and the action which is started at one
or the other point. The easiest way for the child to begin is to
lie facedown with his legs out straight. Turn his head to the right
and place his hands on the floor next to the shoulders. Push the
floor with his left hand to turn to the right. You may have to
push your child at first to give him the idea of the movement.
Push his right shoulder under his body as you pull his left
shoulder up and over. You will both be pleased as he ends up
on his back. To roll to the left, turn his head to the left, and
push with his right hand to start the rotation.

The child:	You put child through movement	Child aids you	Child does himself
1. Head roll			
2. Head lift			
3. Head lift and front roll			
4. Bilateral arms			
5. Bilateral legs			
6. Bilateral arms and legs			
7. Alternating arm			
8. Alternating leg			
9. Alternating arm and leg			
10. Bilateral arms over head			
11. Alternating arms over head			
12. Arms cross body			
13. Arms together			
14. Leg lifts — alternating			
15. Leg lifts — both			

To roll from back to front, place the child on his back with his legs straight and his arms at his side. To roll to the left he should turn his head to the left, push the floor with his right foot while he brings his shoulders and arms to the left at the same time he rotates his hips to the left side. He will end up on his stomach facing left. Next, have him turn without using his foot. You may have to aid him with the rotation, but fade your help as quickly as possible.

After the child has learned to roll from back to front, encourage him to complete several rolls. It may be difficult for him to roll in a straight line if there is inadequate rotation between shoulder and hips. Place a tag at the edge of the floor or mat in a straight line from his hand position to see if he can roll directly to it. Stimulate his shoulder and hips of the roll so he is tactually aware of the parts to be moved.

Log Roll

The child lies at the starting point or at one end of the mat with his arms straight above his head and touching his ear. He rolls about six feet or the length of the mat and then back in the opposite direction to the starting point.

The child:	You put child through movement	Child aids you	Child does himself
1. Body roll, stomach to back			
2. Body roll, back to stomach			
3. Body roll in straight line			
4. Body roll length of mat			
5. Body roll length of mat and back			

Sitting

The child needs to be able to control his head balance before he can learn to sit. Although he can be propped prior to the time he learns to lift and balance his head, you should not try to teach him to sit independently until he has learned to hold up his head and balance it.

Creeping

After the child has learned alternating movements of his arms and legs and has enough head control and balance to sit, he can be introduced to creeping. The easiest way to teach him

The child:	You put child through movement	Child aids you	Child does himself
1. His head lags when pulled to sit			
2. Pulls to sit — raises head			
3. Tips sideways when propped			
4. Falls forward when propped			
5. Slides forward when propped			
6. Sits well when propped			
7. Sits alone briefly when propped			
8. Sits well			
9. Comes to sitting position			

to creep is to get on your hands and knees directly over him. You will be in position to move his arms and legs or lift him if he should need it. Put him through the movements, but be sure to let him do what he can. Encourage him to go through each step by himself. Do not let him become dependent on you for his movements.

Most children learn to get up on their hands and knees and rock their bodies before they learn to creep. This action helps them to build the balance, strength and endurance necessary for creeping. If the child has not attained the hands and knees position, teach it before attempting the creep.

Walking

Before the child learns to go from creeping to walking he

The child:	You put child through movement	Child aids you	Child does himself
1. Arms collapse and legs extend from creep position			
2. Completes creep motion if you move one arm and leg			
3. Creeps on hands and knees			
4. Creeps rhythmically with alternating hands and knees			
5. Keeps back level			

must perfect his balance. He will have to learn to pull himself up and to sit down from a standing position. He will need to stand alone, take alternate steps, and keep his balance at the same time. Walking, then, involves many skills.

Strengthening the Basic Skills

After the child has learned to sit, creep and walk, many activities can be introduced to strengthen these skills.

Rolling sit-ups. Have the child lie on his stomach with his legs straight and hands palms down by his shoulders, face to the right. Push with the left hand into a roll and continue into a sitting position.

Hands and knees roll. The child lies on his back with his hands at his side. Complete a roll to the stomach but continue to raise the body up on the hands and knees.

Hands and feet roll. Begin with the child on his back. Have him complete a roll to his stomach but keep the arms and legs stiff so he comes up on his hands and feet.

Leg strengthening. Have the child lie on his back with his knees bent and his feet against an immovable object. Have him push against the object to move his body.

Twisting. Place hands on hips and rotate upper part of body while lower part remains stationary. Twist to right, then left. Go slowly, then fast.

The child:	You put child through movement	Child aids you	Child does himself
1. Pushes up on arms to sitting position			
2. Completes pull to stand if positioned on one leg			
3. Pulls with arms -- unable to position legs			
4. Pulls to stand			
5. Supports weight on legs			
6. Stands			
7. Has erect posture			
8. Body parts aligned			
9. Feet parallel			
10. Head centered and balanced			
11. Weight evenly distributed			
12. Chest held up			
13. Buttocks tucked in			
14. Knees relaxed			
15. Walks in side step pattern holding on			
16. Walks holding on with both hands			
17. Walks with one hand held tightly			
18. Walks			
19. Touches heel to ground			

	You put child through movement	Child aids you	Child does himself
20. Weight rolls from heel to toe			
21. Feet lift off ground each step			
22. Toes point forward			
23. Arms swing opposite to legs			
24. Supporting leg is straight			
25. Face is forward			
26. Walks straight line			

Bending. Bend each part of the body to the part next to it: head to chest, face to upper arm, thigh to stomach, lower leg to back of thigh, foot toward lower leg. Bend at slow and fast speeds. Bend two body parts at the same time.

Creeping patterns. Hand- and footprints can be cut out of felt, cloth or paper and placed on the floor in various patterns. The child then follows the patterns. Encourage the child to watch his hands as they touch the patterns; this will help his eye-hand coordination. Crawl backward, forward, sideways, in patterns of circles, squares and triangles, and on the knees and elbows.

Seat walk. Have the child sit with his legs extended and his hands folded across his chest, then creep across the floor with his buttocks.

Knee walk. The child kneels with hands at his side. Have him walk forward, backwards and sideways on his knees with his hands remaining at his side.

Arm walk. The child sits with his back to the direction he will be moving. His legs are straight in front of him. His hands are on the mat or floor a little to. the back of his hips. Without using his buttocks or legs; he pulls his body across the mat by only using his two arms together.

The child:	You put child through movement	Child aids you	Child does himself
1. Shows leg strength			
2. Twists			
3. Bends			
4. Creeps patterns			
5. Seat walks			
6. Arm walks			
7. Knee walks			

Running

The child should walk well before running is attempted because of the additional balance required. You may want to run with him at first, holding one hand before he tries it alone.

Jumping

Children normally love to jump and will practice jumping from a bottom step, off boxes, sofas; anything that looks relatively safe to them. To make a good jump, the child should use both feet on takeoff. He should use and control his entire body as he leaves the ground, swinging his arms back as the legs bend, and bringing them up as the legs extend. To effect the best control when he lands, his legs should be about shoulder width apart, either parallel to each other or one ahead of the other. His knees should be slightly bent so his legs absorb the landing shock. His whole body, including his head and arms can help in making the landing light and easy and to keep his balance. His arms should come down naturally when he lands. After the child has learned to jump, he can jump in place and jump from various heights.

The child:	You put child through movement	Child aids you	Child does himself
1. Pushes off with back foot			
2. Leans forward			
3. Lands on balls of feet			
4. Bends elbows about 90°			
5. Swings arms from shoulders			
6. Arms move in opposition to legs			
7. Swings arms straight in front			
8. Points toes forward			
9. Maintains rhythm			
10. Lifts knees			

Cut footprints out of felt, cloth or paper and place them on the floor. Place them so the child will jump forward, backward, and sideways to land on the footprints. They can also be placed so that he can make a succession of forward and backward jumps. It would also be desirable for him to learn to jump forward, backward and sideways over a height such as a two-by-four, as well as jump in the air and make one-fourth and one-half turns.

VARIATIONS. Keeping correct posture, have the child walk up an incline, turn around and return. He can also walk and run forward and backwards up the incline and roll back down.

Place an object about fifteen feet from the child. Have him creep, walk, run, skip and hop forward, backward and sideways to get the object. Try this with a beanbag on his head. Objects can be placed in his path so that he has to make a figure 8 to go around them to reach his goal. The distance can be as varied as the object used.

Balance

Balance is important in order to accomplish all forms of gross movement. If your child is having difficulty with balance in any of the activities, it will help to spend some time working on that aspect alone. How is his standing balance? Can he stand with his feet parallel? Feet close together? Heel to toe? Can he remain in a balanced sitting position without using his hands for support?

SIDE BALANCE. Have him lie on his right side with right arm on the floor straight above his head and touching his ear. His left arm should be straight down the side of his body. His legs should be straight, one on top of the other. Do the same with the left side.

SITTING BALANCE. Do not let your child sit in a position with his legs forming a W. This position provides easy balance for him. Instead, have his legs crossed in front of him, Indian style, or have his legs straight out in front of him. After he has learned to balance himself fairly well, gently push him on the shoulders to see if he can adjust and regain his balance to keep from tipping over. At first warn him of what you are going to do. Later, make a game of it to see if he can keep his balance when taken gently by surprise.

HAND AND KNEE BALANCE. Have the child get into a creeping position. See if he can maintain his balance when he lifts up a leg, a hand, and then a hand and opposite leg at the same time.

KNEE-FOOT BALANCE. Have the child kneel on one knee with his other leg extended in front of him. The extended heel can touch the floor for added balance.

STANDING BALANCE. Have the child stand with one knee held high and both arms folded across the chest. Close both eyes. After he is able to do all three actions, combine them in various ways, such as standing on one foot with his eyes closed and arms folded across the chest. Have the child stand on his tiptoes while you count to ten. Have him stand on one foot to the count of five. Have the child place his hands on his hips, feet apart. Then have him rock forward, backward and sideways. He will need to lift his toes or heels from the floor to maintain his balance.

ELEPHANT WALK. The child bends from the waist with his arms dangling limply. Then he walks forward, taking big steps.

FROG SQUAT. The child squats down with his hands on his hips. One leg is straightened in front of him. As he hops on his bent leg, the other leg is bent and he lands on it while he straightens the first leg in front of him.

CRAB WALK. The child sits with his hands on the floor behind him. He raises his body so it is supported by his hands and feet. Have him then move backward, forward and sideways.

BALANCE BOARD. The use of a balance board will help your child develop his balance because the board will tip each time the child moves, and he will have to balance himself on it or slip off. You can make the board yourself with scrap lumber. The round board requires more balance ability, but a square board can be used if you have no means to saw a round one. The round one should be thirteen to fifteen inches in diameter, with a three-inch circle of wood the same thickness as the board nailed to its center or on the under side. At least one-half-inch plywood should be used. The square one should be a foot square with a three-inch square piece of wood nailed in the center on the under side. Start to use the board by having the child step on the board, stand, and then step back. Next, step on the board with the first foot and then step off the opposite side with the other foot. Stand on the board and tip forward, backward, sideways, turn halfway, turn all the way, bend over to pick up an object, reach to grasp an object, throw and catch a ball. Make it fun!

WALKING BOARD. Some children become quite fearful when they have to walk on a raised surface. Don't you be fearful and add to a fear that already exists or even create one! If your child is fearful, make a pathway on the floor by using folded newspapers or by marking off the floor with masking tape. You may have to start with quite a wide path, but you can narrow it as he becomes able to walk it. By the time he is able to walk a four-inch path he should be able to walk on the balance board.

A ten-foot two-by-four can be used for the board. Two-inch by four-inch pieces can be cut and nailed to the bottom at intervals to raise the board slightly off the floor. You can put nonskid tape on the top of the board to prevent slipping, or sand can be sprinkled on fresh paint to make a nonslip surface. Many different exercises can be used on the board. Check off the list as the child learns to:

1. Walk forward, one foot in front of the other, arms straight out at side.
2. Walk backwards with arms out at side.
3. Walk forward to the middle, turn around, and finish the trip walking backwards.
4. Walk forward, turn sideways and walk to end.
5. Walk forward with right foot always in front of left.
6. Walk forward with left foot always in front of right.
7. Walk backward with right foot always in front of left.
8. Walk backward with left foot always in front of right.
9. Walk forward with hands on hips.
10. Walk backward with hands on hips.
11. Walk forward with arms folded across chest.
12. Walk backward with arms folded across chest.
13. Walk forward, pick up beanbag from the middle of board.
14. Walk forward to center, kneel on one knee, rise and walk to end.
15. Walk forward with beanbag balanced on head.
16. Walk backward with beanbag balanced on head.
17. Walk forward, pick up beanbag, place on head and walk to end.
18. Walk forward to center, step over a stick held twelve inches above the board, continue to end.
19. Walk backward and step over stick.
20. Walk forward under a stick held three feet above the board.
21. Walk backward under the stick.
22. Walk backward with arms straight in front.
23. Walk forward with arms straight in front.
24. Walk forward with arms straight overhead.
25. Walk backward with arms straight overhead.
26. Walk forward, stepping over obstacles on board.
27. Walk forward, hands clasped behind the body.

28. Walk forward, arms out with palms down and a beanbag on the back of each hand.
29. Walk backward, arms out with palms down and a beanbag on the back of each hand.
30. Walk forward, arms out and palms up with a beanbag in each hand.
31. Walk forward to the middle, kneel on one knee and straighten the other leg, rise and walk to end.
32. Walk backward, arms out and palms up with a beanbag in each hand.
33. Walk backward to the middle, kneel on one knee and straighten the other leg, rise and walk to end.
34. Hop forward on right foot
35. Hop forward on left foot.
36. Hop backward on right foot.
37. Hop backward on left foot.
38. Hop forward on right foot to the middle, turn around and walk backwards to end.
39. Hop forward to the end on left foot, turn and hop back.
40. Hop forward to the end on right foot, turn and hop back.
41. Walk left side forward, turn in the middle and walk right side forward.
42. Walk forward with hands clasped behind body.
43. Walk forward with hands clasped behind body to the middle of board, turn and walk backward to the end of board.
44. Walk backward, arms to the back, with beanbags on backs of hands.
45. Walk forward to the center with beanbag on head. Step over a stick held twelve inches above the board, walk to the end.
46. Walk forward, eyes closed.
47. Walk backward, eyes closed.
48. Walk sideways, eyes closed.
49. Have two children start at opposite ends, pass in middle without leaving the board, and walk to the ends.
50. Walk forward on feet and hands.

51. Hold the child's legs and have him walk forward on his hands.
52. Walk on the floor, straddling the board.

You will think of other activities to use on the balance board as you and your child check off his accomplishments. When you notice a particular weakness, develop additional tasks that will strengthen them.

LADDER WALKS. Place a ladder flat on the floor. Think of various ways the child can use the ladder for balance, for help to pick up his feet as he walks, and for the development of general movement. Activities might include

1. Walking forward with one foot on each side of the the ladder.
2. Walking backward with one foot on each side of the the ladder.
3. Walk forward by stepping in the spaces between the rungs.
4. Walk backward by stepping in the spaces between the rungs.
5. Walk forward on the right rail of the ladder.
6. Walk backward on the right rail of the ladder.
7. Walk sideways on the right rail of the ladder.
8. Walk forward by stepping on each rung.
9. Walk backward by stepping on each rung.
10. Walk forward and pick up a beanbag between each rung.

Special Adaptations for the Blind

Orientation and mobility pertain to those skills that allow blind children to move around easily and safely. Orientation helps children to learn about the objects around them, and the mobility skills aid children to move about. Both of these are most important for blind children because they cannot achieve independence without them. Our goal for every child is to help him become as independent as possible.

Orientation and mobility training should begin as early as possible. Informal training can help the child to explore his surroundings and move around in them. Later, he can have more

The child:	You put child through movement	Child aids you	Child does himself
1. Side balances			
2. Sitting balances			
3. Hand and knee balances			
4. Knee and foot balances			
5. Standing balances			
6. Elephant walks			
7. Frog squats			
8. Crab walks			
9. Balances on board			
10. Uses walking board			
11. Ladder walks			

formal training by a person trained in this area. There is, however, much that a teacher or parent can do to help him get ready for formal training.

The exercises already given for general coordination, body image, balance, position in space, and locomotion will all aid orientation awareness and mobility skills. These exercises will establish a foundation for the more formal help he will need.

Additional ways in which you can help the child would be to teach him some of these basics.

Use of the Sighted Guide

A person with vision can act as a guide for someone without vision. There are ways this can be done to be of the greatest help to the person with no or very little vision. Give the child verbal descriptions of all objects, and, at the same time, give him a chance to explore them tactually. This will greatly add to his ability to learn landmarks and help him to get about.

To become a sighted guide for a child, stand alongside the

child and face the same direction. Have the child grasp your arm with his thumb on the outside of your arm just above the elbow and his fingers curled on the inside of your arm. He should grasp your arm firmly but not so that it is uncomfortable to you or him. If a child is too short to comfortably reach above your elbow, he can grasp your wrist.

Have the child stand still while you step one-half pace forward. This is the position that you maintain while you walk together. The half-step lead you take will let the child know what kinds of movements you will be making. Practice turning corners and making stops and starts. When the child becomes good at knowing what your movements are, practice running.

In narrow places or going through doors, the child should move *behind* the sighted person so that he does not bump into anything.

Never leave the child in an open space; always place him in contact with a wall, counter or desk. Each child should be oriented to the schoolroom, playground and his home so that he knows the general location of rooms, furniture, and the objects he will need to use.

Dropped Objects

Try to teach the child to listen for the general direction of sound made by a falling object. Have him face the direction of the sound and then, with his hand before his face, palm facing out, have him move one-half step backwards. He should then bend his knees and squat down. He should never bend from the waist because he may bump his head on some object. After he is squatting, have him place his other hand where he thinks the object fell. He then makes small circle movements on the floor with this hand. The circles get bigger until they are as big as he can reach or until the object is found. If he is not successful on the first try, have him move a little and make a new circle, but always be sure the new circle overlaps the old one.

Locating a Chair

When a sighted person helps a blind child to a chair, he should place the child's hand on the back of the chair. This lets the child know the direction the chair is facing. The child can then move to one side to get around the chair, but one hand should remain on the back. The other hand can locate the chair seat. He then keeps moving until he is directly in front of the chair, turns so that his back is to the chair, feels the edge of the seat with the back of his legs, and sits down.

BODY IMAGE

A child must develop an awareness of "self." He needs to know where his body ends and another person's body begins. He must learn what is part of him and what is a segment of a toy or other object. As he grows, he must learn parts of his body and their functions.

The handicapped child often has a poor body image, and he is unable to relate to other objects or positions because of it. A good body image is a sound basis for building the perceptual skills necessary for classroom work.

Body Parts

When you bathe and dress a child you have excellent opportunities for teaching the names of his body parts. As you bathe the child, name the part that you are washing. "Let's wash your arm, let's soap your hand, let's get your fingers clean," etc. You can do the same thing while dressing, "Put your hands in the sleeve, put your legs in the pants, put your toes into the socks," etc.

Identification

Just playing with the child and naming the parts as you touch them will also help him to learn. After he has acquired the names, have him touch the parts as you name them. "Where are your eyes?" "Where is your nose?"

Once the child has learned his body parts, have him identify them when you name parts of your body. "This is my arm; show me your arm." Begin with the most obvious parts of the body and then go to the the less obvious as he learns. If he cannot locate a particular part, touch it and say the name again. Make sure the child can thoroughly identify his body parts without any clues before you assume he knows them. Begin with the following parts:

face	arm
eyes	hand
ears	elbow
mouth	fingers
chin	wrist
neck	legs
chest	ankle
shoulders	knee
stomach	heel
hips	feet
buttocks	toes
back	

BODY PARTS IN SURROUNDINGS. Once the child has learned the names of his body parts, they can be combined in several activities. One would be to touch parts of his body to something around him.

head to table	nose to book
hands to door	ear to towel
elbows to table	shoulder to wall
knees to floor	fingers to book
back to wall	chest to bed
ankles to floor	wrist to chair
mouth to spoon	stomach to table

BODY PARTS IN ACTION. You can also have him carry out some kind of physical activity involving the body parts. Show him first, but then expect him to learn the actions.

clap your hands	turn your head
nod your head	open your mouth
bend your knees	snap your fingers
shake your head	stamp your feet
wiggle your toes	shrug your shoulders

bend your arms   scratch your back
wrinkle your nose   close your eyes
wink your eye

Body Image in Dolls

A paper doll likeness can be made by having your child lie on a large piece of paper or cardboard. Outline his body with a felt pen. Cut out the figure and draw simple features and clothing. Have the child help you to color them appropriately. Place the paper on the wall so he can stand against it to measure his size. If corrugated cardboard is used, the child can dress it with his own clothing as he would a paper doll.

Regular dolls can also be used to identify body parts as well as pictures and models of people and animals.

Collect pictures of body parts to see if the child can identify them.

Draw incomplete pictures of people and animals to see if the child can add the missing parts. Begin this activity by leaving off a very noticeable part, such as the head or arms. Gradually make the missing parts less obvious: an eye, foot or hand.

Body Image in Games

The "Hokey Pokey" and "Looby Lou" are games which emphasize body parts and are also fun for the child to do.

Cut up paper dolls or pictures of people, put them into envelopes, and use them for quiet activities to see if your child can put them together.

Simple puzzles can be made by cutting out pictures of single figures. These pictures can be cut in two and then three pieces. Puzzles of this type should be made by cutting the picture in two pieces by a vertical cut. After the child has learned to put two pieces together, cut a picture in two with a horizontal cut. Then try two horizontal cuts.

Next, cut a picture with one horizontal and one vertical cut, making four pieces. Then try one vertical and two horizontal cuts. Gradually increase the numbers of puzzle pieces, but limit the number of pieces so the body parts are clearly visible to the child.

Body Part Use

Talk with your child about the use of his body parts as you teach him their names. After he has learned the names, see if he is aware of their functions by asking him questions to see if he can supply the proper body part.

I see with my ....
I hear with my ....
I smell with my.........
I chew with my.........
I bite with my ....
I talk with my ....
I clap with my ....
I walk with my ....
I jump with my ....
I run with my ....

Body Image Places

The positions back, front, top, bottom and sides should be learned as they relate to body parts. Have the child point to the place you designate, such as:

Touch the front of your knee.
Touch the back of your head.
Touch the top of your foot.
Touch the side of your wrist.

Body Positions in Space

Language concepts should be learned in combination with body parts so that the child can move in space on command and be able to describe where he is. Concepts such as above, below, over, under, on, between, up and down can be learned as you demonstrate to the child and then have him repeat the movement. Begin with simple directions and gradually make them more difficult as he learns the concepts. (See section on language).

Put your finger *up*.
Put your head *down*.

Put your hands *between* your legs.
Put your elbows *on* your knees.
Put your hands *over* your head.
Put your hands *in* your pockets.

Have the child move to the place you designate.

Sit *under* the desk.
Stand *between* the windows.
Sit *beside* the door.
Sit *under* the table.
Touch the pictures *over* the table.

Then have him stand in relation to objects in the room.

Stand *in front of* your desk.
Stand *with your back to* the window.
Stand *with your side to* the wall.
Stand *beside* the door.

Move a ball to various parts of the room and, if possible, have the child tell you where it is. Otherwise, describe where you have put it.

In front of you.
Behind me.
Beside the chair.
Behind the wastebasket.
Inside the closet.
Next to a book.
On top of a chair.
In a box.

Creeping and crawling over, under, around and through objects also aids your child in learning his position in space. An obstacle course can be set up with articles found in most rooms. Have him squeeze through small openings such as boxes or under chairs, over pillows, around objects, step over boxes or books, step into a circle made of tape or rope, and walk under a stick. The main purpose is to have the child in contact with the floor as well as various objects so he can get the kinesthetic and tactual feedback sensations as he moves, learning to judge the placement of his body in various situations.

Left and right orientations need to be made so the child will learn those directions. The knowledge of right and left as distinct directions is not usually attained until the child achieves a mental age around six years. These activities will help the child develop the left-right concept as he approaches that stage.

A colored piece of yarn tied on his right wrist will help a child remember as he goes through this series of movements.

Show me your right hand.
Show me your left hand.
Show me your right foot.
Show me your left foot.
Walk sideways to the left.
Walk sideways to the right.
Jump to the left.
Jump to the right.
Look to the left of your body.
Look to the right of your body.
Point to your left side.
Point to your right side.
Raise your right hand.
Raise your left hand.
Point to your left leg.
Point to your right leg.
Touch your right eye.
Touch your left ear.
Turn to the left.
Turn to the right.

Your child should learn his body image with joy and delight as you teach him and play with him off and on throughout his waking hours. Your patience and kind persistence in this and all of the other exercises will bring mutual rewards.

Eye-Foot Coordination

To develop eye-foot coordination, the eyes should follow

The child:	You put child through movement	Child aids you	Child does himself
1. Knows body parts			
2. Identifies body parts			
3. Knows body parts in surroundings			
4. Puts body parts in action			
5. Recognizes body parts in doll			
6. Recognizes body parts in games			
7. Knows body part use			
8. Knows body positions in space			
9. Can move in space			
10. Can name position in space			
11. Can use obstacle course			
12. Has left-right orientation			

what the feet do. Various activities can be used to teach this skill. Place a strip of masking tape on the floor in a straight line. Have the child walk the tape, making sure that he watches his feet touch the tape with each step.

Walk forward
Walk backward
Walk sideways
Walk forward, heel to toe
Walk with just the side of his big toes touching the line

Place a bright-colored piece of yarn on the floor to form a wavy line. Have the child walk on the yarn and make sure he watches to see if his feet touch the yarn with each step.

Walk forward
Walk backward
Walk sideways
Jump back and forth over the yarn
Walk forward and touch the yarn with the side of the big toe

Make large square, circular, and triangular shapes on the floor with masking tape. Have the child walk on the tape, watching to see that his feet touch the tape with each step.

Walk around the shapes
Walk within the shapes
Sit down in the shape
Creep around in the shape

Place felt, cloth or paper footprints in different patterns on the floor. Have the child step on each footprint, watching to see that he uses the proper foot to

Walk in a straight line
Walk in a circle
Walk in a square
Walk in a triangle

Place eight-inch squares, circles and triangles on the floor. Have the child step from one shape to another, as he watches to see that his feet make contact with the shapes.

Step from shape to shape
Step to a matching shape
Jump from shape to shape
Jump to a matching shape

Place footprints between rungs of a ladder placed flat on the floor. Have the child follow the footprints, watching his feet all the while.

Walk forward, alternating left and right feet between the rungs.

Walk backward, alternating left and right feet between the rungs.

Walk sideways, alternating left and right feet between the rungs.

Jump forward with both feet in each rung.

Jump backward with both feet in each rung.

Walk forward in some rungs, and backward in others.

Kick a ball with the right foot, the left, and then, lying on the back, with both feet.

The child:	You put child through movement	Child aids you	Child does himself
1. Walks straight line with eye-foot coordination			
2. Walks curved line with eye-foot coordination			
3. Walks large shapes with eye-foot coordination			
4. Walks on footprints with eye-foot coordination			
5. Walks on small shapes with eye-foot coordination			
6. Walks on footprints in ladder			
7. Kicks ball — right foot			
8. Kicks ball — left foot			
9. Kicks ball — both feet lying on back			

RHYTHMIC ACTIVITIES

The use of music to encourage movement is a good way for the child to gain good muscle control and coordination. Teaching body parts through the use of "Looby Lou" and the "Hokey Pokey" has already been mentioned. Other concepts can also be taught through rhythm. Fast music for running, slow for walking, bouncing and jumping can help the child get the idea of the kind of movement he is supposed to be performing. Acting out songs such as "If you're happy and you know it, clap your hands," "This is the way we wash our clothes," and "Put your finger in the air" can be used to teach concepts. Many different melodies can be used and words can be written to teach them specific information. Rhythm instruments can also be used to teach movement, rhythm and coordination.

It may be necessary to put the child through the rhythmic movements. Stand behind him to help him feel the rhythm and the beat that will aid his movements. Fade your help as he becomes more able to complete the movements by himself.

FINE MOTOR COORDINATION

Fine motor coordination usually involves the use of the hands in manipulating objects. Developing a dominant hand and good eye-hand coordination aids this manipulation.

Several skills are necessary for good hand use. The child should be able to fix his eyes on an object and grasp it in one hand, transfer an object from one hand to the other, keep an object in his hand for the desired time, and use the finger-thumb pincer movement to pick up other objects.

If the child is still using a palmer grasp — that it, fingers against the palm — encourage the use of the pincer grasp, finger against thumb. Place objects such as discs or blocks in the child's hand in the pincer position. See if he can place the objects in a jar or box using the pincer grasp.

Eye-hand Coordination

Have the child pick up small objects using the pincer grasp. Pennies, marbles, beans, bottle caps, poker chips, etc. can all be used. Have him drop the objects into a small-mouthed jar or through a small opening in a box. Plastic covers of empty containers of margarine, potato chips, and coffee can be cut with an X, T, or with a small hole. The child can then push the article through the opening and into the container. Molded egg cartons can also be used: turn the carton upside down and cut holes into the bottom.

Playing with pegs and pegboards provides good eye-hand movements for the child. Large pegs with large holes are best to begin with. As the child becomes better able to manipulate the pegs, smaller pegs and boards can be used. Acoustical tile and plastic golf tees with the points cut off make inexpensive peg boards that are very good for the finer movements.

At first, the child may only be interested in the pegs. He will pick them up, perhaps mouth them, and put them back down. Later on he will place them beside each other. Only after he can grasp them well will he be interested in putting them into the holes in the board.

To teach this and most of the other fine motor activities, sit or kneel behind the child. Place your hands over his and put him through the movement, just as you did when teaching dressing skills. Withdraw your support as quickly as the child shows he is ready to progress by himself. He may be able to do one step but not those that lead up to it or those that follow. Be sure you let him do the steps that he can do independently, but do perform the task in sequence.

The child:	Your hand over his	Your hand on his wrist	Verbal or tactual reminder	He does task by himself
1. Places pegs in row on table				
2. Grasps pegs				
3. Removes pegs				
4. Attempts placing (misses holes)				
5. Places in random order				
6. Follows design when placing				

Bead Stringing

This is another activity that helps develop good eye-hand coordination. Bead stringing sets can be purchased commercially, but articles around the house can also be used. A regular shoelace can be used if two inches of the tip of the lace are dipped into fingernail polish a few times and allowed to harden each time. Use a long lace if you have several beads. Beads can be made from empty thread spools. The plastic spools are better than wood for bead stringing because the holes are smoother on the inside.

A wire hanger can be broken or cut and used if the child

has poor coordination of his hands. Straighten a piece of hanger, turn back the ends, and crimp them with pliers to prevent any sharp edges. A child can sometimes insert wire into the spools when he cannot control a floppy string. If wire is used, it should only be used under your direct supervision and should be placed out of reach of the child when you are not present.

After the child is able to string the beads, he should learn to duplicate patterns. You can make a string of beads and have him make one like it. Different colors of fingernail polish can be used to color thread spools if you don't have a box of beads. The child can learn to string beads randomly by color, shape and number, as well as by pattern.

The child:	Your hand over his	Your hand on his wrist	Verbal or tactual reminder	He does task by himself
1. Removes beads from string				
2. Uses palmer grasp				
3. Uses finger-thumb grasp				
4. Puts string through head				
5. Grasps string coming through				
6. Hold string up, beads slide down				

Clothespins

Both regular and pinch clothespins make good eye-hand coordination tools for a child. The regular clothespins are better to start with because they slip over an edge without additional effort.

Use an empty three-pound coffee can. Have the child slip the pins over the top edge, filling up the complete circle of the rim. After he is able to do this, place dots of different colored paint or fingernail polish on the clothespins and at different places around the top of the can. Have the child slip the colored clothespin over the matching color on the can.

Cover the edges of a piece of corrugated cardboard with masking tape. Paint strips of color along the edge. Have the child slip colored clothespins over the matching strips of paint.

Help him to learn to open and close the pinch-type clothespins. When he learns this, have him pick up pencils, crayons, and other clothespins with the pinch-type clothespin. Paint the pinch-type clothespin the same colors as those on the coffee can and corrugated cardboard mentioned above. Have the child pinch open the clothespins and place them over the corresponding colors.

Nuts and Bolts

Putting large nuts on bolts is a good fine motor activity because of the multiple coordination involved. Start with the largest nuts and bolts you can find. Work from behind the child with your hands over his. Put him through the movement of grasping the nut, centering it on the bolt, and screwing it on. Fade your support as soon as possible. As he becomes able, substitute smaller nuts and bolts.

Beanbags

A beanbag is preferable for playing catch with a child who has poor coordination because it is not as apt to bounce out of his hands, but it gives him the same type of eye-hand coordination as catching a ball; he will enjoy more catching success with the beanbag.

Make beanbags of several different sizes. Begin the activity by using the largest, floppiest bag. Do not fill any of the bags so full of beans that they become hard.

Magnets

Picking up objects with a magnet offers good eye-hand coordination, and many variations can be used for this activity. To pick up paper objects, glue metal washers onto the paper or place paper clips on the edges. Make sure that the object to be

The child:	Your hand over his	Your hand on his wrist	Verbal or tactual reminder	He does task by himself
1. Throws bag in the air				
2. Catches it				
3. Throws from one hand to other				
4. Catches it				
5. Throws to another person				
6. Catches when it is thrown back				
7. Throws bag into wastebasket				

picked up is not heavier than the strength the magnet can support.

Tie the magnet to the end of a string and wrap the other end of the string around a short stick, such as a Tinker Toy,® to make a fishing pole. Have the child fish for the pieces of paper and pick them up with the magnet.

Small metal objects can also be used if you have a strong enough magnet. The small cars that can be purchased by the bag make good items because of the variety of colors and the games that can be played. For example, the fishing pole now becomes a crane. After the child has learned to pick up objects he can then be asked to pick up specific items, shapes or colors.

Cutting

The use of scissors involves good motor skill as well as eye-hand coordination. Scissors are now available with an extra set of handles so you can have the child's and your hands on the scissors at the same time. If you use regular scissors, still work from behind the child, with your hands over his. Guide the paper and the scissors so the cutting edge of the scissors is at a right angle to the paper. Otherwise, the scissors will not cut.

The child:	Your hand over his	Your hand on his wrist	Verbal or tactual reminder	He does task by himself
1. Twirls scissors — no interest in cutting				
2. Holds cutting edge at right angle to paper				
3. Holds one handle in each hand to cut				
4. Holds paper in one hand				
5. Holds scissors in other hand				
6. Moves thumb and fingers to make short cuts				
7. Cuts strip from paper				
8. Cuts along line				
9. Cuts out simple shapes				

CHAPTER 4

ADAPTIVE BEHAVIOR

A DAPTIVE BEHAVIOR can mean many things. It is used here to refer to the perceptual and conceptual development that will allow a child to adapt to preacademic settings. For example, assume that a child is in a room with a large Big Ben® alarm clock. He doesn't know it is there. His eyes are strong enough to see it, his hearing is good enough to hear it ticking, and he has the ability to reach out and feel it, but he doesn't know it's there. His senses do not perceive, or tell him, that it is there. Now let us assume that he is aware that the clock is there. What does he think about it; that it is something that goes "tick, tick, tick" and tells time? If this is so, he would then have a beginning concept, or knowing, of a clock.

The importance of perceptual and conceptual development for the severely handicapped may be enhanced when we reflect on how much the average person looks at things and does not see them, how much he hears and yet is not aware of sound, and how much goes on around him that he filters out and is never aware that it happened.

EYE CONTACT

In order for a child to establish good perception, he must be aware of what is going on around him. He should be aware of all his senses, his environment, toys and the adults around him. Sometimes handicapped children reject their environment and have to be taught to relate to it. One of the means for doing this is to help him establish good eye contact with the adults in his surroundings.

Before beginning to work in this area, it is important to know the level at which the child is functioning. How much eye contact does he have? Observe the child and check the description that best indicates his level.

    .... There is no indication of any awareness. He treats people like objects. He seems happy as long as he is cared for, but it makes no difference to him who looks after him. He does not seem to recognize his parents or the persons who care for him as being different from anyone else.

    .... There is no eye contact with an adult. He never looks at a person directly. He may demand attention, but he looks away or down when it is given to him.

    .... He may establish momentary eye contact with an adult, but it is more likely that he looks at someone, and when they glance at him, he lowers his eyes.

    .... He may show an interest in toys, but not people. He may examine the toys very carefully and use his vision for this purpose. He does not give the same length of time to examining people.

    .... He may be content to watch a person carry out an activity as long as that person is not trying to relate to him. If attention is given to him, he will withdraw his eye contact or reject the attention.

    .... He seeks out an adult when he needs help. This may be the only time he attempts to relate.

    .... He actively seeks adult attention, and demonstrates cooperation.

If your child is in any but the last category, it may be wise to begin eye contact by starting with simple visual tracking. In this way you can observe whether he may have a visual defect. Begin by using a toy which makes some kind of noise. Move the toy in a large semicircle in front of the child while it makes noise. See if the child at any time attends to the movement. Does he move his head to watch? Did he move his head to the midline of his body only, and then stop? Was he able to follow the toy all the way, and if so, was the movement smooth or did his head pause or jerk about midline? Could he smoothly follow the object in a complete 180° arc?

If you are sure there is fairly good tracking, observe whether the child can see a large moving object and a large stationary object. Does he notice a small moving object? A small stationary object? Even though the child may not want you to notice whether he is watching, careful observation of his eyes will show whether he is tracking the objects.

To teach direct eye contact, begin by sitting directly opposite the child. Make sure you are on the same eye level. Have a reward ready to give to the child if he performs for you. A sip of juice, ringing a bell, a hug, a tiny bite of candy can all be used as rewards. If you use something to eat, make sure it is smaller than bite size. Otherwise you will have to wait for the child to eat it, and he may quickly satiate and no longer perform for the reward.

Hold the reward near your eyes and say, "Look at me." If the child looks, even without direct eye contact, reward him and say "Good boy." Demand more direct eye contact as you go along until you are finally rewarding only a direct glance. Then fade your reward by not giving it every time. Continue until the child is rewarded only by an occasional "Good boy."

Keep a record of the number of times you try each day so that you can see the progress of your child.

The child:	No reward	One to one reward	Occasional reward	"GOOD boy"
1. Does not look				
2. Looks generally without direct eye contact				
3. Looks at the face without direct eye contact				
4. Direct eye contact when you call his name				
5. Direct eye contact when you talk to him				

SITTING FOR TASKS

Some children are hyperactive, and it is difficult to get them to attend to a task long enough to complete it. First make sure the child has good eye contact with you and with objects. When you are sure he can establish eye contact long enough to attend, place him on a chair. Place the chair under the table so he is snug against the table and is limited in his ability to slip out. Moving his chair and the table up against a corner with your chair on the other side will work. Plan and set up the learning situation for him. By such structuring, you aid in cutting down the hyperactivity and help the child attend to a task.

Tactual Awareness

Now that you are sure that your child is visually aware, you will also want to help him be tactually alert. Make a small circle from masking or cellophane tape, sticky side out. Place the tape on the child's face or the back of his hand. Check the sentence closest to his behavior.

.....1. There was no awareness of the tape.

.....2. There was awareness with no attempt to remove it.

.....3. The child tries to shake it off.

.....4. The child tries to rub it off.

.....5. The child removes it with a pincer grasp.

If the child could not use the pincer grasp to take off the tape, place your hand over his and put him through the movement. Repeat occasionally to see if the child has progressed to the next step.

Help the child feel the various objects he plays with. See if he can identify them without looking at them. Then take two familiar, but tactually different objects, and put them in a bag. For example, a soft rubber ball and a hard metal car. See if the child can identify the object he touches before he pulls it out of the bag. After he is able to identify these, gradually add more objects to the bag and repeat the task.

Symbols and Form Matching

When matching, it is best to start with three objects, two of

The child by touch:	Your hand over his	Your hand on his wrist	Verbal or tactual reminder	He does task by himself
1. Discriminates objects				
2. Discriminates shapes				
3. Discriminates size				
4. Discriminates texture				
5. Discriminates number				
6. Discriminates "same" and "different"				

which, perhaps little cars, are identified in size, shape and color. The third object might be a toothbrush. After the child is able to match the cars, you can vary the color, although the two objects should be alike in size and shape. For the next matching step, the size of the objects can differ, a little car and a big car, but the color and shape should be the same. If the child can match the objects when either the size or color differ, you can combine the two sets, such as a little green car and a big blue car, although the shape of the object should remain the same. When the child is able to match articles that have differences in color and size, the shape can then be different; you can have one of the cars a convertible and the other a sedan.

After the child can match similar articles that differ in color, shape and size, he can start matching an object to a picture. At the beginning, the picture should match the object in color, shape and size. Polaroid® pictures of the object are good for this step. Next, vary the pictures, first in size, then color, and then shape. Finally, vary all three, making sure the child is able to match the object to the picture at each stage.

Once the child is able to match the variations, proceed to the matching of two identical pictures. Then vary these pictures in color, size and shape. After he has completed these steps, he is ready for all types of matching activities because he will have the concept of matching.

The child:	Your hand over his	Your hand on his wrist	Verbal or tactual reminder	He does task by himself
1. Matches identical objects				
2. Matches objects differing in color				
3. Matches objects differing in size				
4. Matches objects differing in shape				
5. Matches objects differing in color, shape and size				
6. Matches object to identical picture				
7. Matches object to picture differing in color				
8. Matches object to picture differing in size				
9. Matches object to picture differing in shape				
10. Matches object to picture differing in color, size and shape				
11. Checks choice with sample picture				
12. Looks at random till eyes fall on matching picture				
13. Looks systematically over choice of matching pictures				
14. Compares sample card with each of the pictures				

Practice activities using matching skills: from four colored sheets of construction paper cut two identical pieces of each color. Place one piece of each color in front of the child. Hand him the duplicate pieces one at a time and have him place each one over the piece it matches. Gradually increase the numbers of colors in front of the child.

Place several sheets of colored paper spread out in front of the child. Have the child sort colored blocks and place them on the same colored sheet of paper.

Group the child's own toys by color. Have him place them on sheets of paper the same color.

Paint coffee or potato chip cans different colors or wrap and tape construction paper around the cans. Have the child drop colored blocks or marbles into the cans of the matching color.

Cut two duplicate squares of twelve different colors and paste one square of each color on a piece of cardboard. Then have the child place the other twelve squares over their match.

Draw duplicate outlines of objects with a heavy marking felt pen on three-by-five cards. Have the child match the duplicate cards.

Use a deck of playing cards. Have the child sort them into piles according to red or black color. After he can do this, have him sort them according to hearts, diamonds, clubs and spades. Later he can sort them according to numbers.

Outline and cut out shapes from cookie cutters. Have the child match the cookie cutters to the cut-out shapes.

Have the child sort the silverware into piles: forks, knives and spoons. Regular silverware can be used or different colored plastic ones can be purchased; he can sort them by color as well as shape.

Cut out duplicates of various food pictures and have the child match them. Sources of good pictures are the ads in magazines, the labels of canned goods, seed catalogs, picture dictionaries, and card games.

Buy several sizes of nails. Have the child sort them by size and place them in cans or empty food jars.

Cut out two each of four-inch squares of different material. Place one of each different four-inch squares on a cardboard.

Match the remaining kinds of materials to the cardboard. Different kinds of fur, rubber, wool, cotton, silk, cotton balls, velvet, felt, different grades of sandpaper, cordoroy, chamois, leather, etc. should be used for their tactual as well as visual differences.

Cut out pictures of mother and baby animals. Have the child match the mother to her offspring. You may have to put the child through this activity several times before he will be able to complete it by himself.

The child should learn to match textures such as rough and smooth, as well as temperatures and weights. The procedures given above can be used to achieve this.

Puzzles

The easiest way to teach your child to put puzzles together is to begin with a one-piece objective. Take just one piece out of a simple puzzle and let the child replace it. A completely round piece is best to begin with because the child may not know how to rotate a piece that has corners. Take each piece out separately, one at a time, and let him put it back in. After he has put individual pieces in, see if he can replace two pieces at one time. Then go on to three, but only if he is successful replacing two pieces.

After the child has the idea of replacing parts of the puzzle, progress to a simple puzzle. Put it together as the child watches but leave out the last piece. Let the child place that. Then leave out the last two pieces. Continue in this way until the child is able to put the complete puzzle together. If he has trouble rotating the pieces, guide his fingers around the inside of the hole and on the outside of the pieces. Have him look at his hands while he is doing this. Give him a simple verbal description as he touches the piece, such as, "It's round here, and pointed here."

Imitates Shapes

See if your child can imitate the shapes that you draw on

The child:	Your hand over his	Your hand on his wrist	Verbal or tactual reminder	He does task by himself
1. Places one piece more or less by accident				
2. Rotates piece				
3. Looks and matches contours				
4. Places two pieces				
5. Places three pieces				
6. Complete six-piece puzzle				
7. Completes nine-piece puzzle				
8. Completes twelve-piece puzzle				

paper. Use a felt pen that makes a very visible line. His pen should be larger in diameter than a regular pencil until he develops good fine motor control. There is a sequence in the child's development when he may be able to duplicate one shape and not the others. The normal order of development is a vertical

The child:	Your hand over his	Your hand on his wrist	Verbal or tactual reminder	He does task by himself
1. Copies 1				
2. Copies -				
3. Copies v				
4. Copies o				
5. Copies +				
6. Copies □				
7. Copies △				
8. Copies ◇				

line, horizontal line, v-shape, circle, cross, square, triangle and diamond.

Tracing

Tracing around objects, stencils and outlines provides good perceptual development. As he draws the line and watches what he draws, the child receives training in eye-hand coordination. Each hand is used separately, one to trace and the other to hold the pattern to be traced. Various shapes and sizes should be used for tracing.

Chalkboard

A chalkboard hung on the wall gives the child additional perceptual and conceptual experiences as he uses it. Scribbling with chalk, tracing objects, and drawing shapes are all different experiences when completed against a vertical surface. By standing or kneeling behind the child and directing his motions, you can help make larger movements than he would or could be making on regularly sized paper.

TASTE

Different tastes can be used to give the child additional perceptual experiences. When doing this, only one concept should be introduced at a time. If the concept "sweet" is to be used, "sour" should not be given at the same time. A better experience would be to introduce many sweet flavors: candy, sugar, honey, jelly, etc. Rather than introducing the word "sour" for comparison, the term "not sweet" should be used. Vinegar, pickle juice, and lemon could be used and labeled "not sweet."

After you are sure the child has the concept of sweet and understands this term, then "sour" can be taught. Teach sweet, sour, bitter, salty and spicy.

When developing any training of his senses you must first make sure that the child is aware of the stimuli, the thing you are using, and also that he can tolerate it. In time he should recognize the stimuli as something he has experienced before.

He then should learn to react to the stimuli and be able to decide the purpose or meaning of it. Once he has gone through these steps, he should have the concept of the sense training presented to him.

AUDITORY PERCEPTION: SOUND LOCALIZATION

Just as a child must develop gross motor skills before he can develop fine motor skills, the child needs to perceive gross sounds before he can comprehend fine sound differences. A drum makes a good instrument to start with, because most drum sounds are heard across all the frequencies of sound that are used for speech. This means that most children who have hearing losses will be able to hear something when the drum is beat.

To begin, beat the drum and have the child perform some action to indicate his recognition: clap, place a peg in a board, a disk or a spindle, drop a block in a box, etc. Make it an activity the child enjoys so he will be willing to listen more closely in order to perform. Make sure the child sees you beat the drum. Pair the activity with each drum beat. If he does not know what to do, put him through the movement.

Once you are sure the child hears the drum beat and knows what to do, move behind him. Beat the drum and have the child perform the action.

Repeat this process using different sounds. A piano, autoharp, guitar, cowbell, horn, cricket and ratchet can also be used. Make sure the child is able to hear the sound before you attempt to make the sound behind him.

Once the child is able to listen to several different sounds, have him close his eyes while you make a sound in different parts of the room. Have the child point to the source of the sound before he opens his eyes, and then open them to see if he was right. You may need an extra person at first to work with him on the pointing. If no one else is available to aid you, stand close enough so that you can reach the child to help him point. Move around the child so he hears the sound from all different directions.

Sound Identification

Be sure the child is able to hear the sounds you used for the sound localization exercise. Face the child and make one noise, place the noisemaker down, and point to it. Use all the noisemakers in turn and point to each after using it. Have the child turn his back. Make a noise, then turn him around to see if he can show you what instrument the sound came from. If he cannot, repeat the sound as he watches you. Then have him turn around and try again.

Sound Memory

This task is more complicated and many children will have difficulty with it, but it does aid in developing a sequential memory span. Place several noisemakers in a row in front of the child. Make sure he can identify each as to the type of sound it makes.

The child:	Your hand over his	Your hand on his wrist	Verbal or tactual reminder	He does task by himself
1. Hears the sound and reacts				
2. Hears a variety of sounds and reacts				
3. Identifies the source of several sounds				
4. Identifies two sounds in sequence				
5. Identifies three sounds in sequence				
6. Identifies four sounds in sequence				
7. Identifies five sounds in sequence				
8. Identifies six sounds in sequence				

Turn the child around. Make two sounds. Turn the child back around and see if he can identify which sound was made first and which second. Gradually add the third, fourth, fifth and sixth sound as the child is able. This sound memory span will aid the child in developing sound sequence for speech.

CHAPTER 5

COMMUNICATION

THE LANGUAGE DEVELOPMENT sequence of a normal child begins with the cry at birth and continues until the child speaks complete sentences with correct articulation. He does this without specific language or speech lessons.

The exceptional child may need help to acquire language and speech. A deaf child does not hear the speech of others and does not automatically imitate the sounds and words. A young totally blind child does not see the way that sounds are made (the accompanying facial expressions) and will learn words as abstract items unless he is exposed to the concrete object for which that word stands. A severely retarded child may have trouble processing the language that he hears. His memory span may not be long enough to remember a complete sentence. A child may even have trouble remembering that the d, o, g sounds can be put together to form the word *dog*. It may be difficult for a crippled child to make his tongue, lips, and speech muscles do what he wants. If damage to the brain has caused the crippling condition, the language areas of the brain may also have been injured.

No matter what the handicapping condition or its severity, the goal of parents and teachers should be to help the child to become as verbal as possible. We live in a very verbal society, and a child must have some form of communication to become even semi-independent.

Speech is not necessary for all forms of communication. The baby who cries is communicating without speaking words. The child who comes running to your arms when he hears a loud clap of thunder does not have to tell you in words that he is frightened. He communicates that fact by his actions.

When little children fight they may be communicating because their vocabularies are too limited to carry on verbal battles.

All children will not become highly verbal. The more severely handicapped the child, the greater his chances of not being adequately verbal. However the goal is to help him to become as verbal as possible and to give him some other means of communication if he is not able to talk.

When communicating with a child, remember that there are three parts to the process. The child must receive the message, he must process the message to understand it, and he must express himself in some way to answer. The procedure can be compared to a switchboard operator's job when she places a phone call. She must hear the request and hear it accurately in order to begin the process. After she has received the request, she must process the information. If the number sought is out of state, she must relate the name to information she has learned previously. If the caller asks for New York City she will probably know the routing. If it is to a smaller place that is called infrequently, she will probably have to look up the area code, route, etc. To do this she would relate the information to her prior experience as well as training. After the number has been processed, the operator would act to put the call through. She might respond only through movements or she might also verbally express herself and tell you that she has your party on the line. And so it is with a child. If anything interferes with the reception, processing or expression phase, the child will fail to communicate in the normal manner. It is important to remember this. However, expressive language can take many forms: speech, crying, writing, gestures, signals, signing, fingerspelling, etc. Different situations call for different responses.

The following communication methods are concerned with beginning communication methods for severely handicapped children. The vocabulary you choose to teach the child should be directly related to the child and what he does. He will learn words easier if he knows what they mean and can also use them. The vocabulary is listed according to different types of activities and at the level of communication where the child is functioning. The three basic levels of communication are nonverbal, preverbal, and verbal.

NONVERBAL COMMUNICATION

The child at the nonverbal level is functioning as a very young child. He will have little reaction to words or their meanings.

The nonverbal child is not aware of how he can use language to tell others of his needs. If he wants something he cries. He may have a cry to indicate that he is hungry and a different one that says he is tired. If his mother or teacher interprets the cry as a hungry cry, there is still guesswork involved in trying to find out what the child really wants to satisfy his hunger.

The child may smile as he entertains himself. However, this is the same type of smile that very young babies have. It is not a smile the child gives when he looks directly at you that tells you he is happy. Rather, it is a fleeting smile that is not intended to communicate.

The child who is at this stage of verbal development needs to learn that his needs can be communicated. Although words often mean nothing to the child at this period, it does not mean that you stop talking to him. It means that you must talk to him in simple sentences to stimulate him. It also means that you should match physical movement with the words so the child can develop the concept, the meaning, that the word stands for.

Begin by choosing something the child likes to do! If he likes to be twirled around, this should be chosen. If he likes to be pulled in a wagon, that is the activity to begin with when you start to teach words and their meanings.

Each time you do the activity, give the child the words to accompany it. If the child likes to jump, say "Let's jump," jumping yourself as you say the word "jump." Then take the child's hand, saying the words, "Jump, jump, jump," each time your feet leave the floor.

Another activity might be to have the child bend backwards, and then pull himself up as you hold him in your arms, facing you. You can initiate a signal system for this, telling him, "Fall back," and then blow on him lightly as you help him go back. If you accompany the act with words and blow just as he goes through the activity, you are matching a signal and a verbal cue with the activity.

The goal of the activity is to have him say "Fall back." However, nonverbal children do not use words. Therefore the goal is to have him use nonverbal means to communicate his wants and needs. By blowing on his face or neck each time you go through the activity, you hope that he will get the idea and that sometime he will blow on you to let you know that he wants to fall back.

To develop this signal system in nonverbal children, begin by using signals you know the child will be able to perform. Blowing slightly, clapping, jumping, arm positions, and all kinds of signs can be signals that can communicate the child's wishes.

Establishing a daily routine can also help the nonverbal child develop a communication system. He will learn that his physical comfort is often attended by certain activities that happen on a routine basis. The discomfort of wet diapers in the morning can be eliminated by someone's changing him when he awakens. The empty feeling in the stomach is gone after eating. The tired feeling disappears after sleeping. By pairing the routine physical discomforts and comforts with the routines of the day, the child can learn to anticipate what will happen by the physical feelings he has and by the activities that are going on around him. Before too long, the child who sees his mother preparing a meal in the kitchen may climb into the chair where he eats to let her know that he knows his food is coming. Hopefully, when the child becomes hungry, he will climb into his chair to signal that he wants something to eat.

Each time the child signals to you in any way, it is important to reinforce him by giving him what he signaled for. This will be his reward. Let him know that you are pleased so that he will signal again.

Tugging and pulling are also signals that a child can use. If you are always bringing things to the child, you are not only discouraging his exploring behavior and the things he can learn from exploring, but you are also preventing his seeing the source of his satisfaction. He needs to learn that he can get milk from the refrigerator, water from a faucet, graham crackers from a box in the cupboard, and a bell from the toybox.

Therefore, be sure to let him follow you around as you care for his needs. Talk to him as you do it. "Let's get the milk from the refrigerator. Let's take a glass from the cupboard. Let's pour the milk." Hopefully the child will be forming associations in his mind. By showing him the source of things that satisfy him, you can also be building up nonverbal communications.

In time the child may pull or tug you, or vaguely push you to the source of what he wants. When he first begins to signal in this way, you should reward him immediately by showing him you understand and by giving him what he has asked for.

In time, the child may be encouraged to signal specifically for what he wants. Each time he pushes or leads you to the refrigerator to let you know he wants something inside, take time to have him show you what it is inside that he wants. Open the door and take out items one at a time and have him indicate the one he desires. Later on, he can lead you to the refrigerator and place your hand directly on the object he wants.

Every step the child takes in signalling his needs to you is an improvement over a lower means of communication. Don't let the lack of verbal language discourage you. We all had to go through a nonverbal period before we started talking. Keep talking to the child, but encourage him to develop his signalling system.

Eventually, he may be able to signal quite sophisticated messages. When you go into the kitchen to prepare lunch, he may take out the bread, peanut butter, jelly and a knife and hand them to you. He still may have no verbal language, but he is communicating, nevertheless.

The child is able to communicate his needs by:

	Never	Sometimes	Always
1. Crying			
2. Crying differently for varying reasons			
3. Anticipating daily routines			
4. Tugging, pulling, pushing about			
5. Leading people			
6. Placing people's hands on objects			
7. Participating in physical situations			

PREVERBAL COMMUNICATIONS

The child at the preverbal level is beginning to understand that actions and objects have verbal labels. He may give signals one time and imitative babbling behavior another time. However, the one fact that differentiates him from the nonverbal child is that he is beginning to understand that a symbol, or word, can stand for an object or action. The nonverbal child must have an object in his presence in order to refer to it. If it is out of his vision, it does not seem to exist. The nonverbal child is unable to substitute a word for it. The preverbal child is gradually beginning to do this. If the nonverbal child is thirsty, he may lead someone to a faucet, the source of water. The preverbal child will communicate that he is thirsty by gesturing in some way, perhaps by drinking from an imaginary glass, to let you know that he wants something to drink.

The goal of preverbal instruction is to encourage the use of abstract symbolization, written and spoken words, to stand for concrete objects and actions.

The child should be reinforced for any vocal utterances that he makes when he points to communicate his needs. Encourage him to imitate the sounds he hears. If he is vocalizing, imitate the correct sounds back to him to see if he will repeat them. Make a game out of the imitations. Make it fun, and reinforce him so that he will keep trying.

If the child makes calling sounds to you, answer the calls. If he wants you to come to him and indicates this with some kind of noise, go to him immediately. In this way he will learn that he can get your attention by making calling sounds. In other words, he is learning to communicate in abstract ways. He doesn't need to seek you out and pull you where he wants you to go: he can verbally get you there.

At this point the child is probably at the stage where he uses his hands to help him communicate. He has the idea that he can communicate with others, but verbally he is not ready to carry on conversations. You must reinforce every attempt he makes at verbal communication and at the same time encourage him to communicate in other than verbal means. It is the *idea* of communication that is important.

The child may mix his verbal calls with gestures. He will call to get your attention and then hold out his arms for you to take him. He will call and when you turn to him, he shows you a toy he is enjoying. At this stage, the gestures will refer to the immediate situation. The child is learning that a symbol (a gesture) can stand for a concrete object or action. He needs to try out the concept in many ways. Be sure to reinforce him each time he tries to communicate with you with his gestures.

When a child is able to gesture well in the presence of objects, try to get him to gesture about an event that has happened sometime before or a more abstract idea that cannot be communicated by concrete objects in the immediate surroundings. Again, however, you should make sure that the vocabulary used is within the experience of the child and the event to be portrayed is one that he is familiar with. A ride in the car, a trip to the doctor's, or a visit to grandmother are experiences that a child can share.

The child may gesture only single words at the beginning, but eventually he may learn to gesture complete sentences, paragraphs and stories. Remember to reward him for his verbal attempts and to watch carefully as he gestures so you will catch his meaning. He is learning to communicate!

The child is able to communicate by:	Never	Sometimes	Always
1. Pointing			
2. Pointing, accompanied by vocal utterances			
3. Making call sounds			
4. Gesturing to objects or actions in the immediate situation			
5. Gesturing with reference to past objects or actions			
6. Gesturing with reference to more abstract ideas			
7. Gesturing a sentence			
8. Gesturing a paragraph			
9. Gesturing a simple story or complete thought sequence			

Signing

Some children will remain at the preverbal stage. They have the idea that their needs can be communicated, but they will remain on a level below that of a fully verbal child.

Signing is systematized gestures. By teaching the same gestures to preverbal children, it enables them to communicate with each other. Those who are in charge of these children and care for them will not have to learn separate signs for different children. Books containing standard signs are available from some public libraries and from the Gallaudet College Bookstore in Washington, D.C.

There is a controversy about the teaching of signs to deaf children. Philosophies regarding this practice vary in different parts of the country. In the case of older, severely handicapped youngsters, particularly retarded children with extensive brain damage, some system of communication must be established. Then, too, if the language center of the brain has been injured, the child may learn some words but will not be able to use them enough to communicate his needs. Signs can be learned, however, and should be taught if the child is not able to go through the preverbal stage to the verbal stage.

To teach the child a sign, choose an action or object that he enjoys. He will be more willing to learn something with which he has fun. Match the object or action with the sign as frequently as you can so the child will learn to associate the sign and the object in meaningful ways. Let's choose the sign for "eat" as an example. Each time the child eats, you pair the action with the formal sign. Make sure the food is in front of the child and give him the sign as he takes a bite of food. Use the eat sign with different foods so he doesn't get the idea that the sign stands for just one specific food. It may be a while before the child responds to your sign. Do not give up! The child will need time to make the association. Keep pairing the sign with eating and give him the sign each time he eats.

When he does begin to make the association, the child will start focusing on your hand as you sign. It will appear as though he is seeing your sign for the first time. He is now beginning to make the connection between the sign and the food in front of him.

Later, he will know that the sign and eating go together. He will actually wait for you to make the sign, and he may push your hand just to get you started. Be sure to show him that you are pleased with any attempt he makes to recognize what you are teaching.

Once he has made the connection and starts to anticipate your movement, he will be ready to begin imitating you. He will push your hand to make the sign and then try to imitate what you have done. In time, he will imitate your movements when you coax and urge him to do it. Eventually he'll do it by himself. Later, the presence of food will start his sign spontaneously.

VERBAL COMMUNICATION

The child who makes vocal utterances, call sounds, and gestures is on the way to verbal language. He should be encouraged in every way by your responding to any language he presents. A child can be encouraged in this achievement by having him imitate gross body movements. These movements can be refined more and more so that they become in time, fine speech movements.

Imitation

Rather than beginning with speech, begin with the idea of imitating a movement. This can be fun for the child and for you. A whole sequence of gross motor movements can be used. Stand with your hands at your sides while you face the child. Then put your hands out to the sides to see if the child will imitate you. A simple verbal command, "Do this," when you do the activity will give the child the idea of what you want from him. Reward him when he does it.

Once the child has grasped the idea of imitation of these gross movements, move to finer types of movements. Frequently, touching the part of the mouth you want the child to move will help him.

When the child is moving his tongue, he should keep his chin still. You may have to help him by holding his chin while he moves his tongue up and down. The movements need to be separated because separate, distinct movements make good movements for sound production.

If the child is able to imitate movements and has the ability to move his tongue from one position to another to make sounds, he is ready for words. Choose specific words for him to learn. The words should be chosen because they relate directly to him and what he does. The name of the new object will be as difficult for him as a name given to you the first time in a foreign language. The word should be one that is frequently used so once he learns it there will be many opportunities in daily activities for its use.

The following list of vocabulary words relate directly to

The child:	You put child through movement	Child aids you	Child does himself
1. Arms out at sides			
2. Arms out at side, right arm higher			
3. Arms out at sides, left arm higher			
4. Arms up beside ears			
5. Legs spread			
6. Left leg in front			
7. Right leg in front			
8. Right arm out at side			
9. Left arm out at side			
10. Clap hands			
11. Slap knees			
12. One hand at side, touch it with opposite hand			
13. Kneel down			
14. Kneel on one leg			
15. Touch toes			
16. Shake heel			

the child. Starred items are those which are used most frequently and should be taught first. Remember that the child may not immediately use the words you are using. He may have to receive them repeatedly for a while before he can express them. Do keep talking, however, using the words over and over with patience. When the child does respond, don't worry if the sounds aren't all correct. He is communicating, and you can worry about correct sounds later. Be sure to reward him every time he tries.

Some of the exercises included for vocabulary training have been presented for teaching self-care skills and motor ac-

The child:	You put child through movement	Child aids you	Child does himself
1. Wink eyes			
2. Open and close mouth			
3. Stick out tongue			
4. Touch tongue to top lip			
5. Touch tongue to bottom lip			
6. Touch tongue to side of mouth			
7. Touch tongue to opposite side			
8. Move tongue in and out			
9. Move tongue up and down			
10. Pucker lips			
11. Retract lips			

tivities. These exercises are presented now because the teaching emphasis is on building the child's vocabulary and his concept of words. Both receptive and expressive activities are given.

The child:	Child makes movements	Child makes sound when asked	Child imitates immediately
1. Say "ah"			
2. Say "puh"			
3. Say "tuh"			
4. Say "kuh"			
5. Say "ah, ah, ah"			
6. Say "puh, puh, puh"			
7. Say "kuh, kuh, kuh"			
8. Say "puh-tuh, puh-tuh, puh-tuh"			
9. Say "puh-tuh-kuh, puh-tuh-kuh, puh-tuh-kuh"			

Receptive ability comes before the expressive, so many children will be able to perform only receptive tasks. By continuing work with him, hopefully he will progress to the expressive tasks.

VOCABULARY

Body Image

The child's body is a beginning point to teach vocabulary because it is always with and part of him and because he needs to know about himself. For convenience, his body is always there to talk about. A child is very self-centered, and knowledge about himself is very important to him. Begin with the starred vocabulary items. After the child has learned these body parts, the more detailed ones can be introduced.

*Head**
  beard
  chin
  cheek
  ears*
    lobe
  eye*
    eyebrow
    eyelash
    eyelid
    tears
  face*
    forehead
  hair*
  mouth*
    gums
    lips
    saliva
    teeth
    throat
    tongue

mustache
nose*
  nostril
scalp
temple
*Neck**
  throat
*Arm**
  elbow
  forearm
*Hands**
  cuticle
  fingers
  knuckle
  nail
  palm
  thumb
Upper arm
  bicep
Wrist
Trunk

Back	skin
spine	stomach
breast	waist
buttocks	*Leg**
chest	ankle
genitals	calf
anus	foot
penis	arch
vagina	instep
hip	heel
rib	nail
shoulder	toe
side	

ACTIVITIES.

1. *Receptive language.* Bathe the child. As you wash the various body parts, name them.

   Expressive language. After you are sure the child knows the parts of his body, tell him to "Give me your arm," as you wash him. Then ask him which part you should bathe next, and have him name the part.

2. *Receptive.* Use pieces of masking tape. Name the parts of the body as you place tape on them. See if the child is tactually aware of the sensation.

   Expressive. Ask the child, "Where is the tape?" Have the child name the body parts as he pulls the tape off them.

3. *Receptive.* Have the child close his eyes. Then touch a part of his body. See if the child can touch the same place.

   Expressive. Have the child name the part you touched.

4. *Expressive.* Sing songs naming various parts of the body, "This is the way we wash our hands (arms, feet, legs), wash our hands, wash our hands."

   Receptive. Have the child point to the various body parts as you sing the song.

5. *Receptive.* Play "Simon Says" using parts of the body. "Simon

says, 'Put your hands on your head,' " etc.

Expressive. Let the child be Simon.

Self-help

Much of the child's day is spent eating, dressing, bathing and toileting. Vocabulary used while engaged in self-help skills is meaningful vocabulary. Learning the words that symbolize concepts will allow the child to communicate his needs to you. Remember to begin with the starred items and add the other words only after you are sure the child understands and can correctly use the starred items.

Foods

Name the different kinds of foods as the child eats them. If you are helping the child learn to feed himself, talk as you direct each spoonful. "Let's take a spoonful of potato." "Now a spoon of applesauce." "Now some meat." All of this can help the child to associate different tastes with different foods.

ACTIVITIES.

1. *Receptive*. Identify one food in all its forms: a whole orange, a sliced orange, orange sections, orange juice, etc. Prepare the fruit in front of the child and let him taste it as you work with it.

   Expressive. Have the child name the food as he tastes it.

2. *Receptive*. Show the child a piece of sliced fruit. Have him choose the whole fruit from which it came. For example, sliced bananas come from a whole banana, not an orange or an apple. Begin by having the child choose a slice that comes from one of two whole pieces. Gradually add more whole fruit so that the selection becomes more difficult.

   Expressive. Have the child name the sliced fruit as well as each whole fruit.

3. *Receptive*. Mix a gelatin dessert or drink mix. Talk about the color as you add the water to it. Have the child drink it while you identify the flavor.

   Expressive. Have the child tell you what he is doing: opening the package, emptying it, adding water, stirring, etc.

4. *Receptive.* Place several kinds of fruit in a paper bag. Ask the child to choose a fruit tactually.

   Expressive. Have the child name the fruit as he feels each one, pulling it out from the bag to check whether he was right.

5. *Receptive.* Try foods with different tastes and consistencies. Be sure you try only one kind of food at a time so the child does not become confused by two or more different concepts at the same time. Try sweet (honey, sugar, syrup, candy), sour (pickles, sauerkraut, lemon, grapefruit), hard (apples, potatoes, carrots), soft (cottage cheese, whipped cream, marshmallows), etc.

   Expressive. Have the child name either the taste, the consistency, or the food. As soon as he is able to do so, have him tell you all three, adding the color if he knows it. It may help to try the food with the child and make facial expressions that go with the food as well as saying the word. Pucker when you bite the sour lemon, crunch as you bite the hard carrot, and lick your lips with the honey.

Utensils

Begin with the most commonly used items and gradually add the names of the others.

bowl	napkin
dish	plate
cup	saucer
fork	spoon
glass	tray
knife	

ACTIVITIES.

1. *Receptive.* Place two utensils in a paper bag. Have the child identify them tactually, pulling out the one for which you ask. Gradually add more utensils.

Expressive. Have the child name the item he feels and then pull it out to see if he is correct.

2. *Receptive.* Tell the child to "pour." Practice pouring rice and later water from a milk carton into a glass. If the child is blind, have him extend the index and middle fingers of his other hand over the edge of the glass. Have him pour the rice or water over the tips of those fingers so he will know that the rice or water is going inside the glass. Have the child stop pouring when the rice or water reaches his fingertips. Make sure the water is cold or warm when you first use it for pouring. Lukewarm water cannot be felt easily. *Expressive.* Have the child describe what he is doing.

3. *Receptive.* Help the child set the table. Name each utensil as you place it.
Expressive. Have the child name the utensils as they are placed.

4. *Receptive.* You name the appropriate utensil for eating various kinds of food: soup, meat, milk, pudding, etc.
Expressive. Have the child choose the appropriate utensil and name it.

5. *Receptive.* Tell the function of a utensil as you point to it.
Expressive. Have the child point to it and name the utensil as you describe its use: "You put milk in it," "You put it in your lap," "You cut with it," etc.

Grooming

Begin with the starred items and later add the others.

after-shave lotion	nail file
bathtub	perfume
brush*	razor
comb*	scissors
deodorant	shampoo
hand lotion	shaving cream
haircut	shower
nail clipper	sink

soap*	toothpaste*
talcum powder	towel*
toothbrush*	washcloth*

ACTIVITIES.

1. *Receptive.* Tell the child what you are doing as you comb and brush his hair.
   Expressive. Have the child comb and brush his hair, telling what he is doing.
2. *Receptive.* Describe each step as you wash and dry the child's hands.
   Expressive. Have the child describe the process as he washes and dries his hands.
3. *Receptive.* File and clean the child's fingernails. Tell him in a step-by-step way what you are doing and why you are doing it.
   Expressive. Have the child file and clean his nails, describing what he is doing.
4. *Receptive.* Talk about the reason for using deodorant as you help the child apply it. It would be a good idea to do this when you or he really needs it. Have him experience the unpleasant odor, wash under the arms, and then apply the deodorant.
   Expressive. Have the child tell you what he is applying and why as he uses the deodorant. Do not use an aerosol can deodorant. It would be advisable not to let the child handle an aerosol spray can for any purpose until he reaches that stage in his development.

Clothing

Begin with starred items and gradually add others.

belt	bracelet
blouse	buttons
boots	coat*
bra	dress*

earmuffs	sanitary napkin
gloves	scarf
hat	shirt*
hose	shoes*
jacket	shorts*
jeans	skirt*
necktie	slacks
nightgown	slippers
pajamas*	socks*
pants*	sweater
panties*	swim suit
purse	trousers
raincoat	undershirt*
ring	wallet
robe	zipper
rubbers	

ACTIVITIES.

1. *Receptive.* Name all the clothes that the child is wearing.
   Expressive. Have the child name an article of his clothing.
2. *Receptive.* Draw an outline of your child on corrugated cardboard. Cut out the outline. Fill in the facial features and describe what you are doing. Dress the cardboard in clothing belonging to your child, describing your actions.
   Expressive. Have the child tell you the clothing to be placed on his cardboard double. Have him help you dress the figure.
3. *Receptive.* Talk about clothing appropriate for certain activities or weather.
   Expressive. Give specific weather examples and have the child choose the appropriate pictures or articles of clothing. "I wear this when I go to bed." "I wear this in swimming. "I wear this when it's cold."
4. *Receptive.* Put clothing together that do together: undershirt and shorts, socks and shoes, etc.
   Expressive. Choose from two items that which would go with a shoe, pants, skirt, comb, etc. Have the child verbally describe the various combinations: A shoe and sock go together."

5. *Receptive*. Discuss and show the child what clothes are worn on different parts of the body, feet, hands, head, arms, etc.
   Expressive. Have the child tell you what he should wear on different parts of the body.

Household Furnishings

Begin with the starred items and add others as the child is able.

bathtub	pillow case
bed*	plant
blanket	radiator
bookcase	radio
cabinet	record
carpet	record player
chair*	refrigerator*
chest	register
closet*	rug
curtains	sewing machine
desk	sink*
draperies	sheet
drawer*	sofa*
dresser	spread
dryer	stereo
hi-fi	stove
lamp	table*
mattress	television (TV)*
mirror	telephone (phone)*
piano	toilet*
picture	venetian blinds
pillow*	washing machine (washer)

ACTIVITIES.

1. *Receptive*. Slowly name the various furnishings in the room, a few at a time.
   Expressive. Name a particular furnishing. Have the child locate it within the room and name it.

2. *Receptive*. Describe a particular furnishing. Have the child feel it tactually.

   Expressive. See if the child can name the object when he is given only a verbal description.

3. *Receptive*. Name a furnishing and describe its use.

   Expressive. Name a furnishing. Have the child act out or describe its use.

4. *Receptive*. Talk about objects that go together.

   Expressive. Have the child verbally match objects: sheets-bed, desk-lamp, record player-records, pillow-pillow case, etc.

5. *Receptive*. Place doll furniture or pictures of furniture in rooms according to the use of the furniture.

   Expressive. Have the child tell you where to place the furniture.

Discrimination

In order for the child to understand the world around him he must be able to know and interpret what he sees, hears, smells, tastes and feels. He must have words to name those sensations.

Some children do not learn the meanings of, or vocabulary for, what happens to them merely by being exposed to an activity. Therefore, the child must be taught specifically what is meant by the words relating to sensation, shapes, directions, amounts and time.

When teaching a word that has a direct opposite, always teach the one concept to the fullest meaning. For example, dry-wet. A wash cloth before being used is *dry*. During and right after using it, the wash cloth is *not dry*. After dunking a child's hand in water, his hand is *wet*, and after a towel is used, his hand is *not wet*. Teach the opposite vocabulary word *dry* only after you are sure he has the concept *wet*.

Sensory

Teach the starred concepts before the others.

alike	cold*
clean	cool

damp

dry*

different

dirty

hard*

heavy

hot*

light

narrow

rough*

same

smooth*

soft*

spongy

sticky

stiff

thick

thin

warm

wet*

wide

wrinkled

ACTIVITIES.

1. *Receptive.* Demonstrate that one temperature of water is *hot* but the other is *not hot*. Be sure that the water is not hot enough to burn the child. Teach the opposite word *cold* only after you are sure the child understands *hot*.
   Expressive. Have the child supply the appropriate word for the temperature.

2. *Receptive.* Present the various concepts in a tactual, feeling manner. Name them: block of wood (hard) and ball of cotton (not hard), hot water (hot) and ice cubes (not hot), etc.
   Expressive. Have the child name the concepts.

3. *Receptive.* Introduce tactual objects one at a time, making sure the child understands the concept they represent.
   Expressive. Put the objects into a sack. Have the child feel until the child finds a hard (soft, rough, warm) object. Have the child describe what he feels as he touches them.

4. *Receptive.* Verbally describe several objects.
   Expressive. Give the child an object. (hard). Have him match it with other objects (hard, soft, rough).

5. *Receptive.* Point out and have the child touch articles and objects that the child is wearing that are soft (hard, smooth, rough, etc.)
   Expressive. Have the child describe the objects.

Shapes

arch	oval
circle*	rectangle
cane	round*
crooked	short
cube	square*
curve	skinny
cylinder	straight
fat	tall
octagon	triangle

ACTIVITIES.

1. *Receptive.* Guide the child's fingers around the outside edge of one of the shapes. Describe the shape and name it.
   Expressive. Hand the child a shape. Have him name it while his fingers follow the pattern of the shape.
2. *Receptive.* Describe various objects in the room according to their shapes: the ball is round, the table is square, the picture on the wall is oval, the floor is a rectangle.
   Expressive. Have the child describe the objects according to their shapes.
3. *Receptive.* Name a shape. Name objects in the room with that shape.
   Expressive. Play a game, "I'm thinking of something round." See if the child can identify the object.
4. *Receptive.* Place shapes of objects on top of larger objects with the same shape.
   Expressive. Have the child place the shapes and name both the shapes and objects.

Directions

The vocabulary should also be used during the motor activities. The concepts that the vocabulary stands for are essential for good mobility. Begin with the starred items.

above	around
across from	back*

before	left
begin	low
behind	last
below	middle
beneath	near
beside	next
between	next to
bottom	north
center	opposite
ceiling	but*
column	outside
corner	over
diagonal	parallel
distant	perpendicular
door*	rear
down*	right
east	row
edge	side
end	south
facing	start
far	top
finish	under*
first	underneath
floor	up*
foreward	wall
front*	west
high	window
in*	

ACTIVITIES. As with the other concepts, only one should be taught at a time. Also, concepts like *up* and *not up* should be introduced first, and then the word *down*. The opposites are introduced only after a concept is firmly established.

1. *Receptive.* Physically put the child through a movement to show the direction.

Expressive. Have the child act out "Stand *up*." "Don't stand *up*." "Put your hand *up*."

2. *Receptive.* Demonstrate with a box and an object. Place the object *in, on, under, in front of* the box.
   Expressive. Ask the child where you have placed the object. Have him place the object in various positions and tell in what position he has placed it.
3. *Receptive.* Stand *on, in front of, behind* your chair. Have the child imitate your position as you tell him the direction.
   Expressive. Have the child tell you to stand in various positions. Make a mistake to see if he catches you.
4. *Receptive.* Play "Follow the Leader." naming the directions as you go through them.
   Expressive. Have the child be the leader and name the positions.
5. *Receptive.* Place footprints on the floor, red for "right" and blue for "left." Say "right," "left" as the child steps on the prints.
   Expressive. Have the child say "right, left" as he steps on the prints.

Measurements

This concept deals with quantity, or how much. Concrete articles should be used to teach the child the concept. Be sure to teach only one concept at a time so that you do not confuse the child. Begin with the starred items first.

all*	half
big*	halfway
cupful	large
dozen	light
each	little*
empty*	long
foot	many
few	medium
full	middle
gallon	mile
glassful*	more*

most	short
none	same*
numbers 1-100	spoonful*
one-quarter	swallow
one-third	tall
ounce	tablespoon
pair	teaspoon
piece	three-quarters
pint	ton
pound	two-thirds
quart	whole
small	yard

ACTIVITIES.

1. *Receptive.* Use empty plastic margarine containers or coffee cans with a plastic top. Cut a hole in the top. Have the child put pegs, marbles, checkers, buttons, into the container until it is *full*. Empty the container part-way and then all the way to show that it is *not full*.
   Expressive. Have the child describe what he is doing. Ask him as he fills the container, "Is it full?" "Is it not full?"
2. *Receptive.* Have the child hold and feel *big* and *not big* balls.
   Expressive. Have the child describe which balls are *big* and those that are *not big*.
3. *Receptive.* Put different kinds of foods in pill bottles. Have the child taste *some* peanut butter, *some* butter, *some* salt, *some* vanilla, etc. Point out that there is *some* left.
   Expressive. Have the child describe what he has tasted.
4. *Receptive.* Put some pegs in a box. Give *some* or *all* to the child.
   Expressive. Have the child ask for *some* or *all* of the pegs.
5. *Receptive.* Measure two people against each other and point out that one is *big* and one *not big*. Keep comparing people so the child will get the idea of *big* is being a matter of comparison and that something can be *big* one time and *little* the next.

Expressive. Have the child tell which person is *big* and which *not big*. Then use the word *little*.

Time

The passage of time is often difficult for a child. To help him understand something as abstract as learning the concept of time, it should be tied in as much as possible with definite happenings.

after	midnight
afternoon	minute
afterwhile*	morning
age	next
before*	night
beginning	noon
century	on time
day	ordinal numbers
decade	score
early	second
end	slow
evening	start
fast*	tomorrow
finish*	week
hour	year
late*	yesterday
long time	

ACTIVITIES.

1. *Receptive.* Play a record at a *fast* and then a *not fast* speed.
   Expressive. Have the child try to sing *fast* and *not fast*.
2. *Receptive.* Tell what you will be doing in the *morning* and *afternoon*.
   Expressive. Have the child tell what happens in the *morning* and *afternoon*.
3. *Receptive.* Tell what you will do *tomorrow*. Each day discuss the name of the day and the name of *tomorrow*.

Expressive. Mark the day on the calendar. Have the child tell what day tomorrow will be.

4. *Receptive.* Have the child watch and listen to you as you clap your hands and then whistle.

   Expressive. Have the child tell you what you did *before* you whistled.

5. *Receptive.* Put on a coat and button it. Give a step-by-step description of what you are doing.

   Expressive. As you put on the coat, have the child tell you what you must do each step before you do it.

Socialization

Socialization depends on some form of communication. We need to interact and behave with each other in many ways. The more socially appropriate our behavior and interactions are with others, the more we are accepted. Therefore it is important to teach a child the social rules needed to get along with others. The rights and responsibilities of others should be stressed. A child should also know what roles people play and what to expect of people in those roles. He will then be better able to interact with others in appropriate ways.

Amenities

I beg your pardon	may I?
excuse me	please*
I'm sorry*	thank you*

ACTIVITIES.

1. *Receptive.* Use the social amenities vocabulary when talking to the child. Ask him to "please come." Thank him when he hands you things.

   Expressive. Have the child respond to food that is passed at the table with *please* and *thank you.*

2. *Receptive.* Play a "*Simon Says*" game with the addition of the word *please.* If the word *please* is not added, the child is not to do the movement.

Expressive. Have the child be the leader.

3. *Receptive.* Say *thank you* each time you give something to the child.

   Expressive. Have the child say *thank you.*

4. *Receptive.* Pass an object around the table, each person saying, *thank you* when he receives it.

   Expressive. The child joins in by saying *thank you.*

Roles

adult	grandfather*
aide	grandmother*
aunt	grocer
baby*	houseparent
barber	laundryman
beautician	mailman
boy*	man*
brother*	milkman
bus driver	mother*
child	niece
clerk	nephew
cook	nurse
cousin	policeman
dentist	principal
doctor	sister*
friend	teacher*
father*	woman
fireman	uncle
girl*	

ACTIVITIES.

1. *Receptive.* The vocabulary becomes more meaningful when it relates to specific people. Point out that each person has a name and a role.

   Expressive. Have the child name the various persons and give their roles.

2. *Receptive.* Discuss the differences between boys and girls. Point out boys and girls.

Expressive. Have the child tell if he is a boy or a girl.

3. *Receptive.* Say your name and your role. Do this with several people who are familiar to the child.

   Expressive. Give a name. Have the child ask or tell you his role (father, mother, teacher, etc.).

4. *Receptive.* Name all the people in the class or family and tell if each is a boy, girl, man or woman.

   Expressive. Have the child name the people and say what they are.

5. *Receptive.* Show pictures of people important in the child's life. Give their names and their roles.

   Expressive. Have the child select the pictures and name the people and their roles.

INDEX